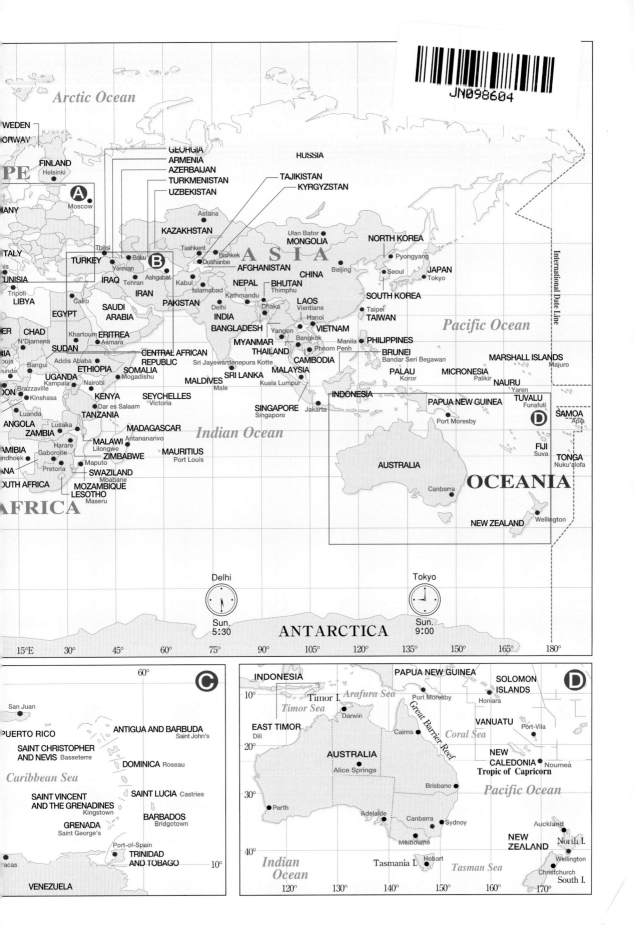

Open Seas

for Global Friendships II

監修　上智大学名誉教授　吉田　研作
　　　上智大学教授　　　藤田　保

BUN-EIDO

CONTENTS

LESSON STEPS

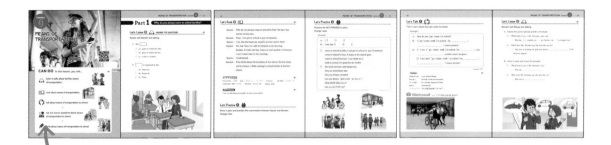

CAN-DO
listen / read / talk / ask and answer / write
LESSON のテーマにそって，**聞く / 読む / 話す / 質問をやりとりする / 書く** 練習の目標です.

▶ Part 1

Let's Listen ❶ 🎧
ANSWER THE QUESTIONS
  D テーマに関連したモデル会話を聞いて質問に答え，内容を理解します.
    会話のあとで〈質問文〉が英語で読まれます.

Let's Read ❶ 📖
  D 前ページの Let's Listen 1 を文字で確認し，内容を理解します.
Words & Phrases
    Let's Read を理解するための語句や表現
KEY PHRASES
    Let's Read の注目表現

Let's Practice ❶❷ 👥
  D KEY PHRASES などをペアやグループで練習します.

Let's Talk ❶ 💬
  R モデル会話を使い，相手に質問したり，自分自身のことを話す練習をします.
Toolbox
    Let's Talk で話すための語句や表現

📷 **What do you see?**
  R 写真に写っている人物や内容について，説明をしたり，話し合う活動をします.

Let's Listen ❷ 🎧
  D Let's Listen 1 より長めの会話を聞いて，質問に答え，内容を理解します.

Let's Read ❷ 📖
  D 前ページの Let's Listen 2 に関連した英文を読み，質問に答えます.

Let's Write ✏️
  R 指示に従って，自分自身のことなどについて書く練習をします.

Let's Talk ❷ 💬
  R 書いたものをペアやグループでやりとりします.

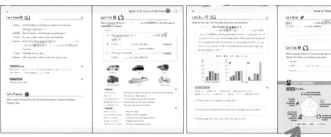

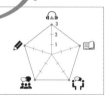

🏃 **CHECK YOURSELF**

LESSON の終わりに, 5項目の自己評価 (3段階)
"CAN-DO チェック" を行いましょう.

▶ Part 2

Let's Listen 🎧
ANSWER THE QUESTIONS

D Part 1 Let's Listen 1よりやや情報量の多いモデル会話を聞いて内容を理解します.
会話のあとで〈質問文〉が英語で読まれます.

Let's Read ❶ 📖

D 前ページの Let's Listen を文字で確認し, 内容を理解します.

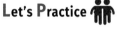
Let's Read を理解するための語句や表現

KEY PHRASES
Let's Read の注目表現

Let's Practice 👥

D KEY PHRASES などをペアやグループで練習します.

Let's Talk ❶ 💬

R モデル会話を使い, 相手に質問したり, 自分自身のことを話す練習をします.

Let's Talk で話すための語句や表現

Let's Read ❷ 📖

D 少し長めの英文を読み, 質問に答えます.

Let's Write ✏️

R 指示に従って, 自分自身のことなどについて書く練習をします.

Let's Talk ❷ 💬

R 書いたものをペアやグループでやりとりします.

 … Let's Listen, Let's Read, Words & Phrases, KEY PHRASES, Toolbox には音声があります.
D … Display 度の高い活動：質問に対する答えを知った上で, あえてまた質問し, それに答えるような活動.
R … Referential 度の高い活動：新たな情報を知るために質問し, それに答えるような活動.

MAIN CHARACTERS

Friends & Teachers

Asakura Sayaka

Koyama Yumi

Noguchi Ayame

Honda Nanami

Uchikawa Kana

Honda Kentaro

Honda Nanami

Honda Kentaro

Honda Family

Mika

Yutaka

Maya & Coco

Hara Rikuya

Sakamoto Hayato

Eric Chen

Hara Shinya

Kimura Shizuka

Oliver King

R L

English

Ueno Takashi

mathematics

Mori Haruko

mathematics

Jon

Meg

Taylor Family

Tony

Mandy

Ryan

BUSINESS

SMARTPHONE/TABLET

● アクセス方法

A-1 右のQRコードを読み取るとOpen SeasⅡ
のトップページにアクセスできます.

A-2 トップページ,または画面右上のメニュー ☰
をタップし,はじめたいLessonを選択します.

B 各Lessonとも,一番はじめのCAN-DOページ写真
右下にあるQRコードを読み取ると,そのLessonに
アクセスできます.

A-1 　A-2 　B

1 CAN-DO

各LESSONの目標を確認しましょう.

7 CHECK YOURSELF

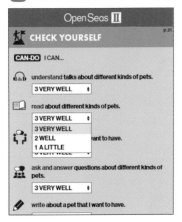

　3段階で自己評価を行い,その
結果を先生やクラスメイトと共有
しましょう.

2 Let's Listen

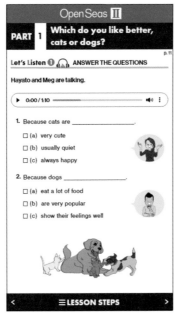

モデル会話を聞いて質問に答え
ましょう.

3 Let's Read

Let's Listenを文字で確認(Let's
Read①)したり,Lessonのテーマ
を扱った英文(Let's Read②)を
読んだりしてみましょう.

How to Use Open Seas with Your Smartphone / Tablet

4 Let's Practice

OpenSeas Ⅱ

PART 1 Which do you like better, cats or dogs?

p. 13

Let's Practice ❷

Work in pairs and talk about different kinds of pets.

< Example >

A: Which do you like better, mice or squirrels?
B: I like mice better than squirrels because mice are cute and easy to look after.

mice　squirrels　rabbits　hamsters

parrots　owls　tropical fish　turtles

are cute / can talk / are not noisy / are quiet / are more beautiful / are easy to take care of / are expenve

≡ LESSON STEPS

ポイントとなる表現の練習を
しましょう.

> Which do you like better, cats or dogs?

5 Let's Talk

OpenSeas Ⅱ

PART 1 Which do you like better, cats or dogs?

p. 14

Let's Talk ❶

Work in pairs and talk about cats and dogs.

< Example >

A: Which do you like better, cats or dogs?
B: I _____.
A: Why?
B: Because _____

Toolbox

▶ 0:00 / 1:10

とてもおとなしい	very quiet
とてもうるさい	very noisy
世話しやすい	easy to look after
世話しにくい	hard to look after
賢い	clever
…を散歩に連れて行く	take ... for a walk
…を散歩に連れて行く必要が ない	don't have to take ... for a walk

≡ LESSON STEPS

自分自身のことについて,
ペアやグループでやりとり
する練習をしましょう.
Toolboxの語句を参考にして
練習しましょう.

> Why?

> Because they're very quiet.

6 Let's Write

OpenSeas Ⅱ

PART 1 Which do you like better, cats or dogs?

p. 16

Let's Write

Which do you like better, cats or dogs? Why?

COPY

≡ LESSON STEPS

COPY をタップし, 入力した
内容を email, SMS などで送信
しましょう.

A PET AS A FAMILY MEMBER

CAN-DO In this lesson, you will...

 listen to talks about different kinds of pets.

v

 read about different kinds of pets.

v

 talk about a pet that you want to have.

v

 ask and answer questions about different kinds of pets.

v

write about a pet that you want to have.

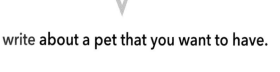

Part 1 — Which do you like better, cats or dogs?

Let's Listen 1 ANSWER THE QUESTIONS 🔊

Hayato and Meg are talking.

1. Because cats are ☐☐☐

   ☐ (a) very cute

   ☐ (b) usually quiet

   ☐ (c) always happy

2. Because dogs ☐☐☐

   ☐ (a) eat a lot of food

   ☐ (b) are very popular

   ☐ (c) show their feelings well

Let's Read 1 📖 🔊

Hayato : Hi, Meg. May I ask you something about pets?

Meg : Sure.

Hayato : Which do you like better, cats or dogs? Both of them are very popular pets.

Meg : I like cats better than dogs.

Hayato : Why?

Meg : Dogs often bark and are very noisy. But cats are usually quiet. How about you, Hayato?

Hayato : I like dogs better because they show their feelings when they are happy. I like to play with them.

Meg : I think cats show their feelings, too.

Hayato : Yes, but they are often hard to understand.

Words & Phrases 🔊

bark ほえる   **noisy** うるさい, やかましい   **quiet** おとなしい, 静かな   **show...** …を表す
feelings 感情   **hard to understand** 理解しにくい

KEY PHRASES 🔊

Which do you like better, 〜 or ...?
I like 〜 better because....

Let's Practice 1

Work in pairs and practice the conversation between Hayato and Meg.
Change roles.

Let's Practice ❷ 👬

Work in pairs and talk about different kinds of pets.

〈Example〉

> A : Which do you like better, mice or squirrels?
>
> B : I like mice better than squirrels because mice are cute and easy to look after.

mice	squirrels	rabbits	hamsters
parrots	owls	tropical fish	turtles

are cute / can talk / are not noisy / are quiet / are more beautiful / are easy to take care of / are expensive

Let's Talk ❶

Work in pairs and talk about cats and dogs.

〈 Example 〉

A : Which do you like better, cats or dogs?

B : I _____ .

A : Why?

B : Because _____ .

Toolbox

とてもおとなしい	very quiet	…を散歩に連れて行く	take... for a walk
とてもうるさい	very noisy	…を散歩に連れて行く必要がない	don't have to take... for a walk
世話しやすい	easy to look after	芸をたくさん覚えることができる	can learn many tricks
世話しにくい	hard to look after	…を室内で飼うことができる	can keep... indoors
賢い	clever		

📷 **What do you see?** Look at this photo and talk about it.

Let's Listen ❷

Maya and Shinya are talking.

1. Check the correct boxes.

ペット	a cat	a dog	世話の種類			悩み・問題点		
Shinya	☐	☐	①☐	②☐	③☐	④☐	⑤☐	⑥☐
Maya	☐	☐	①☐	②☐	③☐	④☐	⑤☐	⑥☐

①

give food to my [cat/dog]

②

walk my dog

③

brush my [cat/dog]

④

very noisy

⑤

very sleepy

⑥

scratch my hands

2. Work in pairs and check the answers.

(1) What pet does [Shinya/Maya] have?

—— [He/She] has _____.

(2) What does [Shinya/Maya] do for [his/her] pet every day?

—— [He/She] _____ _____ ,

(3) What is a problem with [his/her] pet?

—— [His/Her] pet _____.

Let's Read ❷ 📖 🔊

Read a story about pets in Greentown and answer the questions.

> In Greentown, dogs are the most popular pet. Some people like large dogs such as golden retrievers because these dogs are strong and friendly. Other people like small dogs such as toy poodles. These dogs are popular because they are cute and easy to look after. Some of these pet owners meet in parks every morning and exchange information about their dogs.

Words & Phrases 🔊

golden retriever ゴールデンレトリーバー   **toy poodle** トイプードル   **pet owner** ペットの飼い主
exchange... …を交換する

1. Why do some people like large dogs?

   _____ .

2. Why are small dogs popular?

   _____ .

3. What do some dog owners do in parks every morning?

   _____ .

Let's Write

Which do you like better, cats or dogs? Why?

_____

_____

Let's Talk ❷

Work in pairs. Talk about which you like better, cats or dogs, and why.

Part 2 What animal do you want to have for a pet?

Let's Listen ANSWER THE QUESTIONS 🔊

Hayato and Meg are talking.

1. ☐ (a) A hamster because it is cute

   ☐ (b) A parrot because it can speak

   ☐ (c) A tropical fish because it is beautiful

2. ☐ (a) A cat because it is friendly

   ☐ (b) A large dog because it is strong

   ☐ (c) A small dog because it is easy to look after

3. Because they ☐☐☐

   ☐ (a) are not noisy

   ☐ (b) are not dangerous

   ☐ (c) do not need any food

⟨ Pet ⟩

large dog   small dog   cat   hamster   parrot   tropical fish   snake

Let's Read ❶ 📖 🔊

Hayato : Hi, Meg. What animal do you want for a pet?

Meg : Well, I want a parrot.

Hayato : A parrot? Why?

Meg : Well, because it can speak. I want to teach it some words.

Hayato : Sounds interesting.

Meg : How about you, Hayato?

Hayato : I want to have a dog, a small dog.

Meg : Not a large dog?

Hayato : No. Small dogs are easy to look after.

Meg : I see. By the way, are you interested in robot pets?

Hayato : Yes. Robot pets don't need any food. How about you, Meg?

Meg : I'm not interested in robot pets because I like real animals better.

Words & Phrases 🔊

for a pet ペットとして　　**parrot** オウム　　**by the way** ところで　　**robot pet** ロボットペット

KEY PHRASES 🔊

What animal do you want for a pet?

I want a parrot.

Why?

Well, because it can speak.

Let's Practice

Work in pairs and practice the conversation between Hayato and Meg.
Change roles.

Let's Talk ①

Work in pairs. Talk about a pet that you want and about robot pets.

〈 Example 〉

A : What animal do you want for a pet?

B : I want _____ for a pet.

A : Why?

B : Well, because _____ .

A : Are you interested in robot pets?

B : Yes. Because _____ .

　　(No. Because _____ .)

large dog	small dog	rabbit	hamster
parrot	tropical fish	turtle	( )

Toolbox

（とても）人なつっこい	（very）friendly
話すことができる	can speak
感情をよく表現できる	can show its feelings well
目がかわいい	has lovely eyes
…と屋内で一緒に遊ぶ	play with... indoors
ロボットペットは高価だ。	Robot pets are expensive.
ロボットペットは病気にかからず、アレルギーの原因にもならない。	Robot pets don't have any diseases or cause allerges.

Let's Read ❷ 📖 ◀))

Read the passage with the graph and answer the questions.

Pets in Greentown

In Greentown, there are many different pets. These days, rabbits and hamsters are becoming popular. Many people are interested in unusual pets such as snakes, but very few families have such pets now. Snakes are often from foreign countries, so they are expensive. Pets are good friends and important family members, but some bad pet owners throw away their pets in parks or rivers. Pet owners should always take good care of their pets.

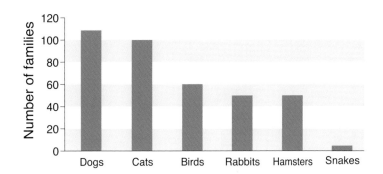

Words & Phrases ◀))

unusual 珍しい   few 少ない   important 大切な

1. Which are more popular in Greentown, birds or hamsters?

_____ .

2. Which pets often come from foreign countries?

_____ .

3. What do some bad pet owners do?

_____ .

Let's Write

What animal do you want to have for a pet? Why?

_____

_____

Let's Talk ❷

Work in groups of three or more. Talk about an animal that you want to have for a pet and why. Tell the class about your group's discussion.

⟨Example⟩

In our group, two students want dogs, one student wants a cat, and one student wants a hamster.

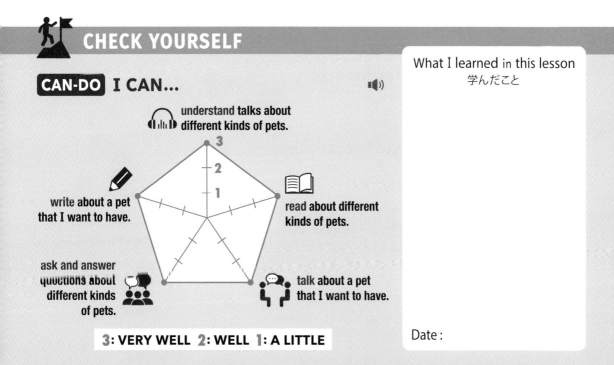

CHECK YOURSELF

CAN-DO I CAN... 🔊

understand talks about different kinds of pets.

3
2
1

write about a pet that I want to have.

read about different kinds of pets.

ask and answer questions about different kinds of pets.

talk about a pet that I want to have.

3: VERY WELL **2: WELL** **1: A LITTLE**

What I learned in this lesson
学んだこと

Date :

Lesson 2

FOOD PREFERENCES

CAN-DO In this lesson, you will...

 listen to talks about food they like or dislike.

v

 read about food preferences.

v

 talk about food you like or dislike.

v

 ask and answer questions about food preferences with your friends.

v

 write about food you like or dislike.

Part 1   I like meat, but I don't like fish.

Let's Listen ❶ ANSWER THE QUESTIONS 🔊

Yumi and Hayato are talking.

1. He likes [   ] .

    ☐ (a) fish

    ☐ (b) meat

    ☐ (c) vegetables

2. Because they don't [   ]

    ☐ (a) look nice

    ☐ (b) smell good

    ☐ (c) taste good

Let's Read ❶ 📖 🔊

Yumi : Hayato, do you have any preferences for food?

Hayato : Yes, I do. I like meat, but I don't like fish.

Yumi : Why not?

Hayato : Fish sometimes smell bad. And some fish don't look so nice, eels for example.

Yumi : Eels? I think they taste good. Are vegetables OK? I don't like carrots and cucumbers.

Hayato : I don't like them, either. I usually leave them on my plate.

Words & Phrases 🔊

preferences 好き嫌い   **smell...** …なにおいがする   **look...** …に見える   **eels** ウナギ

taste... …な味がする   **carrots** ニンジン   **cucumbers** キュウリ   **not..., either** もまた…ない

leave... …を残す

KEY PHRASES 🔊

Fish sometimes smell bad.

I usually leave them on my plate.

Let's Practice ❶ 👬

Practice the conversation between Yumi and Hayato.
Change roles.

Let's Practice ❷ 👫

Work in pairs and talk about food you like or dislike.

〈Example〉

A : Do you like【 ① 】?

B : ［Yes, I do. / No, I don't.］

They【 ② 】. I【 ③ 】.

①	②	③
meat fish --- carrots cucumbers tomatoes green peppers *Other vegetables:*	（don't）smell good look nice taste good *Other reasons:*	usually eat them ［first / last］ never eat them leave them on my plate *Other reactions:*

〈reactions 反応〉

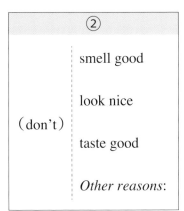

Let's Talk ❶

Talk about your favorite food in pairs.

⟨ Example ⟩

> A： Do you like [curry and rice / ramen / soba / spaghetti / udon] ?
>
> B： Well, I _____ it. _____. How about you?
>
> A： [I like it, too. / I don't like it, either.] _____.

Toolbox

脂っこい食べ物	**oily food**
香辛料を使った食べ物	**spicy food**
塩辛い食べ物	**salty food**
しょう油	**soy sauce**
日本風の味	**Japanese flavor**
安い	**cheap**
栄養価が高い	**nutritious**
早く出てくる。／出てこない。	**It's（not）served quickly.**
幼い頃から親しんでいる	**I'm familiar with it since childhood.**

📷 What do you see?   Look at this photo and talk about it.

Let's Listen ②

Mika and Ryan are talking.

1. Check the correct word and fill in the blank.

（1）What kind of traditional Japanese snacks does Ryan like?

—— He likes ［ □ bitter　□ salty　□ spicy　□ sweet ］ ones.

（2）Why does Ryan like *sembei*?

—— Because _____.

2. Work in pairs and check the answers.

（1）What kind of traditional Japanese snacks does Ryan like?

—— He likes _____.

（2）Why does Ryan like *sembei*?

—— Because _____.

Let's Read ❷ ◀))

Read a report on food preferences in Greentown and answer the questions.

> In Greentown, we found children like tasty, sweet foods better than bitter, sour, or spicy ones. They like foods that are easy to chew and swallow, too. Foods with good memories are often their favorites. They do not like foods with bad smells or a bad appearance. We also found more preferences in children than in adults. If we eat many different kinds of food, we may come to have more favorite foods.

Words & Phrases ◀))

tasty うまみがある　**sweet** 甘い　**bitter** にがい　**sour** 酸っぱい　**chew** かむ
swallow 飲み込む　**memory - memories** 記憶, 思い出　**appearance** 見かけ　**adults** 大人

1. What kind of foods do children like in Greentown?

_____ .

2. What kind of foods do children dislike in Greentown?

_____ .

3. Who has more likes and dislikes about food in Greentown, children or grown-ups?

_____ .

Let's Write ✏️

Write about your food preferences with comments.

_____

_____

Let's Talk ❷

Work in pairs and talk about your food preferences.

Part 2 Why don't you cook yourself?

Let's Listen ANSWER THE QUESTIONS ◀))

Yumi and Rikuya are talking.

1. They're talking about Yumi's mother's ⬜.

- ☐ (a) cooking
- ☐ (b) new business
- ☐ (c) volunteering

2. The problem is Yumi's ⬜.

- ☐ (a) mother changed her mind
- ☐ (b) mother changed her job
- ☐ (c) mother's food doesn't taste the same

Let's Read ❶ 📖 ◀))

Yumi : My mother recently started using frozen and canned foods in her cooking.

Rikuya : Do you mean she has changed her mind about healthy food?

Yumi : No. I don't think so. I'm sure she always cares about our health. She does the cooking herself to give us well-balanced meals. But....

Rikuya : But what?

Yumi : I sometimes feel her cooking's flavor is getting lost.

Rikuya : So, you miss your mother's usual food flavor. I'm sure you will get used to the new tastes soon enough.

Words & Phrases ◀))

recently 最近 **frozen foods** 冷凍食品 **canned foods** 缶詰め **change** *one's* **mind** 考えを変える
care about... …を気にかける **do the cooking** *oneself* 自分で料理する **get used to...** …に慣れる
soon enough すぐに

KEY PHRASES ◀))

I'm sure she always cares about our health.

Let's Practice

Work in pairs and practice the conversation between Yumi and Rikuya.
Change roles.

Let's Talk ❶

Work in pairs and share your opinion about various kinds of food.

〈Example〉

> A : What is your favorite food?
>
> B : I like _____ .
>
> _____ . (*reason/comment*) (**Toolbox**)
>
> A : That's good. What about other food?
>
> B : I don't like _____ .
>
> _____ . (*reason/comment*) (**Toolbox**)
>
> A : Hmm. I'm sure you'll like it someday.

〈someday いつかそのうち〉

hamburger

natto

dried squid

umeboshi

potato chips

fried noodles

fried shrimp

tofu

Toolbox

…にいた時のことを思い出す。	I remember the time I was in....
食べた後で気持ちが悪くなったことがある。	I once became sick after eating [it / them].
試してみたが飲み込めなかった。	I tried once, but I couldn't swallow [it / them].
特別な場合に食べる。	We eat [it / them] on a special occasion.
ほんの少しで満腹感がある。	I feel full with just a little bit of [it / them].

Let's Read ❷ 📖

Read the passage with the graph and answer the questions.

─ Popular Cuisine in Greentown ─

Italian food is the top choice for all ages. That's probably because it isn't very expensive. Chinese food is in third place. It was at the top before. Thai food is regarded as healthy and becoming popular among older generations. On the other hand, Korean food is more popular among younger generations. People say French food is delicious, but it is less popular than before.

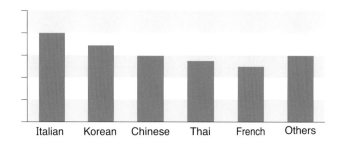

Italian   Korean   Chinese   Thai   French   Others

Words & Phrases 🔊

cuisine （特定地域の文化の）料理   probably おそらく   expensive 値段が高い

the top choice 最も選ばれているもの   for all ages 全ての年齢の人に   Thai タイの

regarded as... …と見なされている   among... …の間で   older generations 上の世代の人たち

on the other hand 一方で   younger generations 若者たち   delicious おいしい

less popular 人気が薄れている   than before 以前より

---

1. What is the least popular food in this graph?

_____ .

2. Which food was at the top a few years ago?

_____ .

3. Why is Thai food becoming popular among older generations?

_____ .

Let's Write

Write about your food preferences with comments.

_____

_____

_____

Let's Talk ❷

Work in groups of three or more and talk about your food preferences. Tell the class about your group's discussion.

〈Example〉

（NAME）_____ likes _____. ［He／She］ doesn't like _____.

_____. （_reason／comment_）

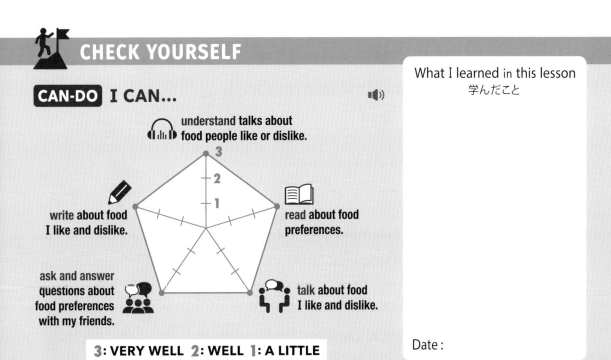

CHECK YOURSELF

CAN-DO I CAN... 🔊

understand **talks about food** people like or dislike.

write **about food** I like and dislike.

read **about food** preferences.

ask and answer questions about food preferences with my friends.

talk **about food** I like and dislike.

3: VERY WELL 2: WELL 1: A LITTLE

What I learned in this lesson
学んだこと

Date :

CAN-DO In this lesson, you will...

 listen to talks about familiar means of transportation.

v

read about means of transportation.

v

talk about means of transportation to school.

v

ask and answer questions about means of transportation to school.

v

 write about means of transportation to school.

Part 1 Why do you always come to school by bike?

Let's Listen ① ANSWER THE QUESTIONS 🔊

Hayato and Nanami are talking.

1. She [   ] .

   ☐ (a) goes to school by bike

   ☐ (b) goes to school by bus

   ☐ (c) walks to school

2. [   ] is important to her.

   ☐ (a) Exercise

   ☐ (b) Fresh air

   ☐ (c) Time

Let's Read 1 📖 🔊

Hayato : Why do you always come to school by bike? We have bus service in this area.

Nanami : Time. I can get to school in just 18 minutes.

Hayato : I see, but the buses are usually on time, aren't they?

Nanami : Yes, but I have to walk 10 minutes to my bus stop. Besides, if I miss the bus, I have to wait another 10 minutes. I can't waste time in the morning.

Hayato : I understand.

Nanami : If we think about the locations of our school, the bus stops and my house, I think coming to school by bike is the best choice.

Words & Phrases 🔊

bus service バスの便   just... ちょうど…だけ   Besides, ... それに加えて…   another... さらにもう…の
waste time 時間をムダにする   location （物のある）場所   choice 選択肢

KEY PHRASE 🔊

I see, but **the buses are usually on time, aren't they?**

Let's Practice 1 👥

Work in pairs and practice the conversation between Hayato and Nanami. Change roles.

Let's Practice ❷ 👬

Practice the KEY PHRASES in pairs.
Change roles.

⟨Example⟩

A : I【   ①   】

B : I see, but【   ②   】

①   come to school by bike. I can get to school in just 20 minutes.

     come to school by bus. It stops at the school gate.

     come to school by train. I can sleep on it.

     walk to school. It's good for my health.

②   the roads are busy and dangerous.

     they are sometimes late.

     they are always crowded.

     can you always [get a seat / sit down]?

     what about rainy days?

     can you get fresh air?

Let's Talk ❶

Talk in pairs about how you come to school.

〈 Example 〉

A : How do you [go / come] to school?

B : I [go / come / walk] to school (by _____).

_____ . (*reason/purpose*)

A : (1) I see. I [go / come / walk] to school (by _____), too.

_____ . (*another reason/purpose*)

(2) I see, but I [go / come / walk] to school (by _____).

_____ . (*reason/purpose*)

〈 purpose 目的 〉

Toolbox

学用品を持ち運ぶ	**carry school things**
環境に優しい	**friendly to the environment**
決まった時間で	**in a certain amount of time**
経済的な	**economical**
…の中で友達と話す	**chat with friends [in / on] …**

📷 **What do you see?** Look at this photo and talk about it.

Let's Listen ❷ 🎧　　　　　　　　　　🔊

Nanami and Rikuya are talking.

1. Check the correct phrase and fill in the blank.

　(1) What kind of car is Ms. Kimura's new car?

　　　—— She has ［ □ a sports car　□ an electric van　□ a compact car ］.

　(2) What does Ms. Kimura say she uses the car for?

　　　—— She uses it to drop off and pick up her ＿＿＿＿＿＿＿＿＿＿ from

　　　nursery school.

2. Work in pairs and check the answers.

　(1) What kind of car is Ms. Kimura's car?

　　　—— She has ＿＿＿＿＿＿＿＿＿＿.

　(2) Why does Ms. Kimura say she uses the car?

　　　—— She uses it ＿＿＿＿＿＿＿＿＿＿.

Let's Read ❷ 📖 🔊

Read an article about the use of cars and answer the questions.

> People use cars for various purposes. Some use cars to save time. They use cars to get somewhere quickly. They do not like waiting for a bus or train. Others use cars to go somewhere comfortably. Cars help us travel with heavy baggage or in bad weather. Still others use cars for pleasure. They enjoy driving and going where they like. Driving a car itself is fun for them.

Words & Phrases 🔊

article 記事   various いろいろな   save 節約する   somewhere どこかへ   comfortably 快適に
baggage 荷物   still others さらに他の人は   pleasure 楽しみ   where they like 好きなところへ
... itself …それ自体

1. Why do the first group of people use cars?

_____.

2. Are there any other purposes people use cars for?

_____.

3. Which group do you think you will be in when you are a grown-up?

_____.

Let's Write ✏️

Write about how you come to school and your reasons.

_____

_____

Let's Talk ❷

Work in pairs and discuss how you come to school and your reasons.

Part 2 How will we go there?

Let's Listen ANSWER THE QUESTIONS

Nanami and her father Yutaka are talking.

1. They're talking about ⬚ .

    ☐ (a) going fishing in the river

    ☐ (b) visiting Yutaka's mother

    ☐ (c) taking a trip by bus

2. Nanami wants to go there ⬚ .

    ☐ (a) by bike

    ☐ (b) by car

    ☐ (c) by train

Let's Read ❶ 📖 🔊

Yutaka :   We're thinking of visiting my mother this weekend.

Why don't you come with us?

Nanami :   Yes, of course, I will. How are we going there?

Yutaka :   By train. I don't want to drive on weekends.

Nanami :   Hmm. How about going by bike? I've always wanted to do it once. It's close enough to cycle. Besides, you can get good exercise.

Yutaka :   That may be true, but....

Nanami :   OK. If you don't want to cycle, let's go by train.

Words & Phrases 🔊

How are we...? どのように…しますか   **I've always wanted to...** 前から…したいと思っていた
cycle 自転車で行く   **close enough to...** 十分…できる距離

KEY PHRASE 🔊

That may be true, but....

Let's Practice

Work in pairs and practice the conversation between Yutaka and Nanami.
Change roles.

Let's Talk ❶

Work in groups of three or more. Discuss what transportation is the best way for weekends or holidays.

⟨ Example ⟩

A : What do you think is the best transportation to take on the weekend?

B : I think _____ [is / are] the best.　　　　　(**Toolbox A**)

_____ . (*reason* / *comment*)

C : That may be true, but _____ [. / ?] (**Toolbox B**)

I think _____ [is / are] good, too.

minivan

taxi

train

sightseeing bus

ferry

electric bike

Toolbox A 🔊

行きも帰りも楽しめる。	We can enjoy ourselves on the way as well as at the destination.
遠方に行ける。	We can go to a distant place.
その場で計画を変更できる。	We can change our plan there and then.
駐車や駐輪の場所を心配しなくてよい。	We don't have to worry about parking.
ひととの接触を避けられる。	We can avoid contact with others.

Toolbox B 🔊

雨が降ったらどうするの。	What if it rains?
必ずしも一緒に座れるわけではない。	Maybe we can't sit together.
時間を気にする必要がある。	You have to be careful about the time.
誰かが運転しなければならない。	Somebody has to drive.
何度も乗り換えをしなければならない。	We have to change many times.

Let's Read ❷ 📖

🔊

Read the passage with the graph and answer the questions.

How People Go to Work in Greentown

On sunny or cloudy days, people in Greentown choose how to go to work simply by the distance and time to get there. However, on windy days, they do not use bikes very much. They probably think it will be harder and can be a little dangerous to cycle against the wind. On rainy days, too, they hardly use bikes. Cars and buses are less popular, as well. It is probably because they don't want to be late for work due to traffic jams.

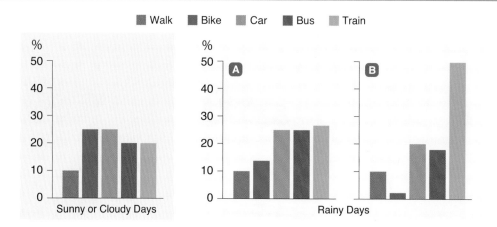

Walk ■ **Bike** ■ **Car** ■ **Bus** ■ **Train**

Words & Phrases 🔊

choose 選ぶ   **simply** 単純に   **distance** 距離   **against the wind** 向かい風で
hardly ほとんど…しない   **as well** 同じように   **due to...** …のせいで   **traffic jam** 交通渋滞

1. Why are bikes not so popular on windy days?

_____ .

2. Which means of transportation to work does not change with the weather?

_____ .

3. Which graph shows the result of the rainy days, A or B?

_____ .

Let's Write

Write how you think someone should go to school if the school is within walking or cycling distance. Give your reasons. 〈within... distance …の範囲内に〉

_____

_____

_____

Let's Talk ❷

Work in groups of three or more and talk about means of transportation to school. Tell the class about your group's discussion.

〈Example〉

(NAME)_____ says [he / she] _____

[because / if / _____.]

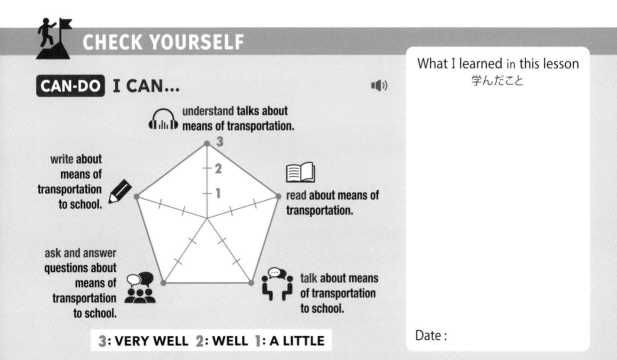

CHECK YOURSELF

CAN-DO I CAN...

understand talks about means of transportation.

read about means of transportation.

write about means of transportation to school.

ask and answer questions about means of transportation to school.

talk about means of transportation to school.

3: VERY WELL 2: WELL 1: A LITTLE

What I learned in this lesson
学んだこと

Date :

Lesson 4

TOO HOT

CAN-DO In this lesson, you will... 🔊

 listen to talks about global warming around us.

v

 read about global warming around us.

v

 talk about global warming around us.

v

 ask and answer questions about global warming around us.

v

 write about global warming around us.

Part 1 We should not stay outside.

Let's Listen ❶ ANSWER THE QUESTIONS 🔊

Ayame and Sayaka are talking.

1. Go to ☐

   ☐ (a) the pool

   ☐ (b) the beach

   ☐ (c) a movie theater

2. Because ☐

   ☐ (a) it is going to be over 35°C

   ☐ (b) Dad can't drive her home today

   ☐ (c) she wants to go to Sayaka's home

Let's Read 1 📖 🔊

Sayaka : Hi, Ayame. I thought you were going to the beach.

Ayame : Dad planned to take us to the beach.

But he changed his mind. It's going to be very, very hot today.

Sayaka : That's right, maybe over 35°C.

Ayame : If it's that hot, we shouldn't stay outside for a long time.

Sayaka : Yes, we should stay home or in another cool indoor place like a library or a movie theater.

Ayame : Well, I was really looking forward to going to the beach. Now, I'm totally bored!

Sayaka : Why don't you come over to my house? Let's watch a movie together.

Ayame : Thank you, Sayaka. You've saved my day!

Words & Phrases 🔊

stay outside 外にいる   You've saved my day. 助かった。

KEY PHRASES 🔊

If it's that hot, we shouldn't stay outside for a long time.

We should stay home.

Let's Practice 1

Work in pairs and practice the conversation between Sayaka and Ayame.
Change roles.

Let's Practice ❷

Work in pairs and give some advice to your partner.
Change roles.

⟨ Example ⟩

> A : It's too hot.
>
> B : Yes. We should [stay home / not stay outside].

| turn off the air-conditioner | often drink water | bring cold water with us | do sports for a long time |

Let's Talk ①

Work in pairs and talk about the hot weather.

〈 Example 〉

A : Ah, maybe it'll be over 35°C today.

B : It's too hot. _____ . (**Toolbox A**)

A : Yes, _____ . (**Toolbox B**)

Toolbox A

これ以上外にはいられない。 **I can't stay outside anymore.**

気分が悪い。 **I feel sick.**

涼しい場所に行きたい。 **I want to go somewhere cool.**

とてものどがかわいている。 **I'm very thirsty.**

Toolbox B

ファーストフード店に行きましょう。 **Let's go to a fast-food restaurant.**

冷たい飲み物を買いましょう。 **Let's buy something cold to drink.**

水を飲んだほうがいい。 **You should drink water.**

エアコンの効いたところに行った方がいい。 **We should go to an air-conditioned place.**

冷たいスムージーを作りましょう。 **Let's make cold smoothies.**

📷 What do you see? Look at this photo and talk about it.

Let's Listen ❷   ◀))

Ayame and Jon are talking.

1. Check the correct phrase.

（1）Where was Jon going to go tomorrow?

—— Jon was going to go ☐ .

☐ （a）to Canada and visit his grandparents

☐ （b）to the airport to see off his father

☐ （c）to see a tennis match with Ayame

（2）Why did Jon and his family change their plan?

—— Because ☐

☐ （a）their flight was canceled

☐ （b）their flight was put off for 12 hours

☐ （c）a big typhoon was coming to Japan

2. Work in pairs and check the answers.

（1）What was Jon's first travel plan?

—— His first plan was _____.

（2）What is Jon's second travel plan?

—— His second plan is _____.

（3）What are Jon and Ayame going to do tomorrow?

—— They're going to _____.

Let's Read ❷ 📖 🔊

Read a story about the weather in Greentown and answer the questions.

> It is very hot this summer in Greentown. It is often over 35°C. That is too hot. This temperature is sometimes dangerous, so many people don't go out. They stay home, drink something cold and relax. But some people are more active. They go to a pool or the beach, swim and enjoy eating ice cream. Anyway, you should often drink water on hot days.

Words & Phrases 🔊

temperature 気温

1. How high is the temperature in Greentown this summer?

_____.

2. What do many people do on hot days?

_____.

3. What do active people do?

_____.

Let's Write ✏️

What would you like to do on very hot days?

_____

_____

Let's Talk ❷

Work in pairs and talk about what you would like to do on hot days.

Part 2   Did you have hot days like this?

Let's Listen   ANSWER THE QUESTIONS

Rikuya and Grandma are talking.

1. ☐ (a) Making shaved ice for her family

☐ (b) Using air-conditioners

☐ (c) Taking a shower later in the day

2. ☐ (a) The temperature

☐ (b) Showers

☐ (c) Shaved ice

Let's Read ❶ 📖

Grandma :   Oh, Rikuya, you didn't go out today. Do you like staying home?

Rikuya :   No, I'd like to go out. But it's just too hot again today.
All my friends are staying home these days, too.

Grandma :   Well, it was over 35℃ every day this week. That's certainly
dangerous for seniors like me. Maybe it's even dangerous
for young people like you.

Rikuya :   Did you have hot days like this when you were young?

Grandma :   No, we had very hot days only in the middle of August.
And the temperature wasn't as high as 35℃.

Rikuya :   Were you OK without an air-conditioner?

Grandma :   Yes. We were quite used to it. And we often took a shower
after it got really hot during the daytime.
That made us feel a little cooler.

Rikuya :   I envy you. The climate has changed a lot.

Grandma :   Yes, it has. Rikuya, I'll make you shaved ice. I always loved
it on hot days when I was young.

Rikuya :   Your shaved ice hasn't changed!

Words & Phrases 🔊

even for...　…にとってさえ　　　hot days like this　こんなに暑い日　　　in the middle of August　8月の中頃

took a shower　シャワーを浴びた　　　That made us feel a little cooler.　そうすると少し涼しくなった。

envy　うらやましい　　　climate　気候　　　shaved ice　かき氷

KEY PHRASES 🔊

Did you have hot days like this when you were young?

The climate has changed a lot.

Let's Practice

Work in pairs and practice the conversation between Grandma and Rikuya.
Change roles.

Let's Talk ❶

Ask your older family members or friends about the summers when they were young. Talk about the difference in the weather.

〈Example〉

> A : Did you have (hot , very hot , extremely hot) days like this when
>
>   you were young?
>
> B : [Yes, (1) sometimes. / No, (1) never.]   (**Toolbox A**)
>
>   The temperature was _____.
>
> A : (2) Were you OK without an air-conditioner?   (**Toolbox B**)
>
> B : Yes. We (3) were quite used to it.   (**Toolbox C**)

〈extremely 極端に〉

Toolbox A 🔊

いつも	always	しばしば	often
ほとんどいつも	almost always	ときどき	sometimes
たいてい	usually	ほとんど(し)ない	rarely, almost never

Toolbox B 🔊

ほぼ一日中外で遊んでいましたか。	Did you play outside almost all day?
海に行きましたか。	Did you go to the beach?
飲み物を持たずに出かけたの。	Did you always carry some water or something to drink?

Toolbox C 🔊

used an electric fan	cooled off on the veranda	ate a slice of cold watermelon (eat-ate)	swam in the river (swim-swam)

Let's Read ❷ 📖 🔊

Read the passage with the table and answer the questions.

Summer of Greentown

In Greentown, it is very hot in the summer. People are beginning to think it is the result of global warming. The average temperature in August is higher than before. And they also have less rain. Sometimes the heat is really hard for everyone. Some people feel sick because of the heat. Greentown is trying to solve the problem. For example, they are planting more trees. They are also sprinkling water over roads in the morning and in the afternoon.

Table: Weather in Greentown in August

	1990	1995	2000	2005	2010	2015	2020	
Average Temperature	26	26	27	28	28.5	30	30.5	℃
Amount of Rain	140	80	80	10	50	70	50	mm

Words & Phrases 🔊

table 表   average 平均の   sprinkle まく

1. What was the average temperature in August in 1995 and in 2010?

_____ .

2. How much rain was there in 1990 and in 2005?

_____ .

3. What are people in Greentown doing to try to solve the problem?

_____ .

Let's Write ✏

Do you notice any global warming around us? Write about it.

_____

_____

_____

Let's Talk ❷

Work in groups of three or more and talk about global warming around us. Tell the class about your group's discussion.

〈Example〉

In our group, one student asked his grandfather and two students asked their mothers about the weather when they were younger.

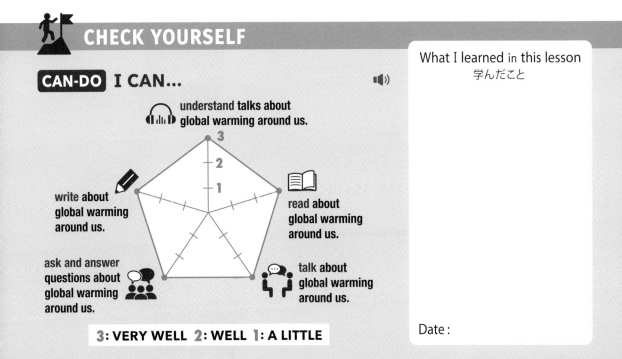

CHECK YOURSELF

CAN-DO I CAN...

understand **talks** about **global warming around us.**

write **about global warming around us.**

read **about global warming around us.**

ask and answer questions about **global warming around us.**

talk **about global warming around us.**

3: VERY WELL 2: WELL 1: A LITTLE

What I learned in this lesson
学んだこと

Date :

Lesson 5

ONLINE MEDIA

CAN-DO In this lesson, you will...

 listen to talks about personal preferences for news sources.

∨

 read about the use of different news sources.

∨

 talk about different news sources.

∨

 ask and answer questions about news sources.

∨

✏ **write** about personal preferences for news sources.

Part 1   I watched a tennis match on the internet.

Let's Listen ❶ ANSWER THE QUESTIONS   🔊

Kana is calling Jack in Australia.

1. Because he ▢ last night

   ☐ (a) had a slight fever and couldn't sleep well

   ☐ (b) stayed up late studying for his tests

   ☐ (c) stayed up late watching tennis online

2. She is ▢ .

   ☐ (a) curious about the contents of online programs

   ☐ (b) not interested in watching TV online at all

   ☐ (c) more worried about Jack's health than watching TV online

Let's Read ❶ 📖 🔊

Kana : You sound very tired today, Jack. What's wrong?

Jack : I watched a tennis match online until very late last night.

Kana : You watched it on the internet?

Jack : That's right. It was the US Open held in New York.

Kana : So, you watched a live tennis match in the U.S. from Australia?

Jack : Right. It's not that difficult.

Kana : I've never watched any TV programs online. How is it different from regular TV?

Jack : You don't need a TV. You can watch them online with your smartphone or computer.

Kana : That's really convenient. I might look for some interesting online programs. But Jack, please take care. You shouldn't stay up late watching TV anyway.

Words & Phrases 🔊

What's wrong? どうしたの。   **not that difficult** それほど難しくない

a live tennis match 生中継のテニス試合   **stay up late** 夜ふかしをする   **anyway** とにかく

KEY PHRASES 🔊

I've never watched any TV programs online.

How is it different from regular TV?

Let's Practice ❶ 🧍🧍

Work in pairs and practice the conversation between Kana and Jack.
Change roles.

Let's Practice ❷

Work in pairs and talk about differences between the following sets.
Change roles.

〈Example〉

> A : How is a keyboard different from a mouse?
>
> B : You type with a keyboard and you use a mouse as a pointing device on the screen.

keyboard / mouse

rain / snow

paper dictionary / electronic dictionary

Let's Talk ❶

Work in pairs and talk about online TV.
Change roles.

〈 Example 〉

> A : How is online TV different from regular TV?
>
> B : You can _____ with online TV.

Toolbox

多くの番組を見る	watch many programs
世界中どこからでも番組を見る	watch programs from anywhere in the world
外国の番組を見る	watch foreign programs
番組にコメントを送る	send your comments to programs
自分で番組を作る	create your own programs
見逃した番組を見る	watch a program you missed

📷 **What do you see?** Look at this photo and talk about it.

Let's Listen 2

Tony and Mandy are talking.

1. What are Tony and Mandy going to do tonight? Choose the correct picture.

Ⓐ

Ⓑ

Ⓒ

Ⓓ

2. Work in pairs and check the answers.

(1) What kind of TV program does [Tony / Mandy] like?

— Mandy likes ______________________________.

Tony likes ______________________________.

(2) Where is [Tony / Mandy] going to watch online TV?

— Mandy ______________________________.

Tony ______________________________.

(3) What kind of rules is Tony's family going to make?

— They ______________________________.

Let's Read ❷ 🔊

Read a story about TV for older people and answer the questions.

> As you know, many young people are watching TV on the internet these days. However, older people are also shifting from regular TV to online TV. A new report from the city says online viewing has increased 35 percent in people 65 and older since last year. This finding shows that older people are not afraid to use new technology.

Words & Phrases 🔊

these days 最近は　　**shift from A to B** AからBに移行する　　**viewing** 視聴　　**increase** 増える

finding 調査結果, 報告　　*be* **afraid to...** …するのを怖がる

1. How do many young people watch TV these days?

_____.

2. How do some older people watch TV now?

_____.

3. What can we know from the report?

_____.

Let's Write ✏️

Do you think online TV will be more popular among older people in the future? Why?

_____

_____

Let's Talk ❷

Work in pairs and talk about the future of online TV with your friends.

Part 2 Do you read news online?

Let's Listen ANSWER THE QUESTIONS 🔊

Jon and Ayame are talking.

1. You can always ☐☐☐☐ .

- ☐ (a) believe them
- ☐ (b) get better information
- ☐ (c) read the latest news

2. ☐ (a) News online is better than newspapers.

- ☐ (b) Jon's parents don't read newspapers.
- ☐ (c) Newspapers are expensive.

Let's Read ❶ 📖 🔊

Ayame : Who reads the newspaper in your family, Jon?

Jon : No one. We watch news programs on TV and check the news online whenever we want. When it comes to information, many people prefer using smartphones or computers these days.

Ayame : But I still see some people reading the newspaper on the train.

Jon : Reading a newspaper is the traditional way to get news, but sometimes the information isn't up to date. A lot can happen in 24 hours.

Ayame : Yeah. That's true. Why do some people still buy newspapers, then?

Jon : That's a good question, but I honestly don't know the answer. Perhaps some people prefer reading the bigger pages of newspapers. And they seem to be enjoying even the action and sound of turning the pages.

Ayame : That's exactly the case with my grandfather. His morning begins with fetching the newspaper from the mailbox and reading it over a cup of tea. He says he's OK without online media.

Words & Phrases 🔊

whenever どんな時でも   **when it comes to...** …のこととなると   **traditional** 伝統的な

not up to date 最新ではない   **can...** …する可能性がある   **fetch...** …を取ってくる

KEY PHRASES 🔊

Who reads the newspaper in your family?

A lot can happen in 24 hours.

Let's Practice

Work in pairs and practice the conversation between Ayame and Jon.
Change roles.

Let's Talk ❶

Work in pairs. Talk about news online.
Change roles.

〈 Example 〉

A： Do you read news online?

B： Yes, I do. / No, I don't.

A： Why?

B： Because _____ .

A： Are you interested in newspapers?

B： Yes. _____ .

（ No. _____ .）

Toolbox

最新情報を得る	get the latest news
どこでもニュースを読める	can read the news anywhere
カラーの写真がある	have color pictures
たくさんの情報を得る	get a lot of information
持ち運びたくない	don't want to carry them with me
買わなくてはいけない	need to buy them
インターネットに接続する必要がない。	There is no need to connect to the internet.
バッテリー不要。	There is no need for any batteries.

Let's Read ❷ 📖

Read the passage with the graph and answer the questions.

News Sources for Americans

The graph shows that TV is a popular source of information for older people in the U.S. More than 80 percent of the people aged 65 and over use TV as a news source, while only 16 percent of the youngest group get information through TV. On the contrary, social media is the major source for young people. More than one-third of the youngest group access social media to get the latest news. The oldest group, however, do not use social media very much. Only 8 percent of this group uses it for the news.

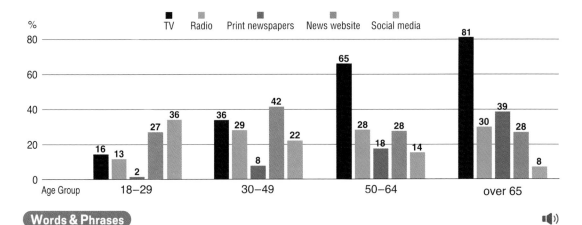

Words & Phrases 🔊

source 情報源　**~, while...** ~である一方…　**through TV** テレビを通じて
on the contrary それどころか　**social media** （SNS,ブログなど個人で情報発信・交換を行う）ソーシャルメディア
major 主な

1. Which news source is the most popular for the oldest group?

_____ .

2. Which news source is the most popular for the youngest group?

_____ .

3. Why do you think there are differences across the age groups?

_____ .

Let's Write

What source do you use to check the news? Why?

_____

_____

Let's Talk ❷

Work in groups of three or more and talk about how you get news. Tell the class about your group's discussion.

〈Example〉

In our group, two students check news on social media, while one student reads the newspaper.

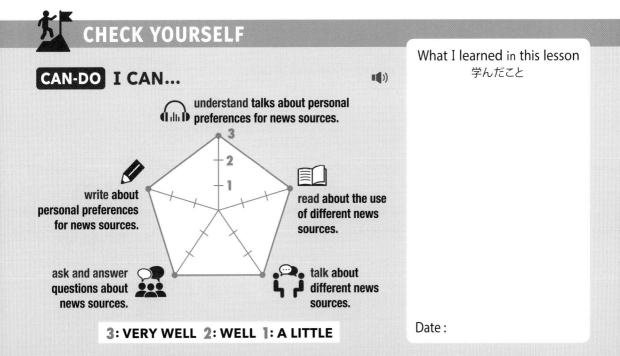

CHECK YOURSELF

CAN-DO I CAN...

What I learned in this lesson
学んだこと

understand **talks about personal** **preferences for news sources.**

read **about the use** **of different news** **sources.**

write **about** **personal preferences** **for news sources.**

talk **about** **different news** **sources.**

ask and answer **questions about** **news sources.**

3: VERY WELL 2: WELL 1: A LITTLE

Date :

WORK EXPERIENCE AND JOBS

CAN-DO In this lesson, you will...

 listen to talks about work experience and jobs.

V

 read about work experience and jobs.

V

 talk about a job that you want to have.

V

 ask and answer questions about different kinds of jobs.

V

 write about a job that you want to have.

Part 1 My school has a work experience program.

Let's Listen ① ANSWER THE QUESTIONS 🔊

Ken and Meg are talking.

1. ☐ (a) Two days

   ☐ (b) Three days

   ☐ (c) Four days

2. Because he wants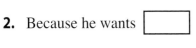

   ☐ (a) to read a lot of books

   ☐ (b) to be a teacher

   ☐ (c) to be a librarian

Let's Read ❶ 📖 🔊

Meg : Hi, Ken. You look excited.

Ken : I am! Next week, I'm going to work at the city library. It's for a work experience program.

Meg : A work experience program?

Ken : Yes. It's a program at my school. Students go to different workplaces. For example, some students work at a nursery school.

Meg : I see. How many days are you going to work at the library?

Ken : Three days. Wednesday, Thursday, and Friday.

Meg : Why did you choose to work at the library?

Ken : Well, I'm thinking of becoming a librarian in the future. This experience will be very helpful for me.

Words & Phrases 🔊

city library 市立図書館　　**work experience** 職場体験　　**workplace** 職場
nursery school 保育園　　**librarian** 司書

KEY PHRASES 🔊

Why did you choose to work at the library?
Well, I'm thinking of becoming a librarian in the future.

Let's Practice ❶ 👥

Work in pairs and practice the conversation between Meg and Ken.
Change roles.

Let's Practice ❷

Work in pairs and talk about work experience and jobs.
Change roles.

〈Example〉

> A : Why did you choose to work at the <u>library</u>?
>
> B : Well, I'm thinking of becoming a <u>librarian</u> in the future.
>
>   *or*
>
> Because I want to be a <u>librarian</u> in the future.

library

nursery school

bakery

hospital

> *be* a nursery school teacher / open a bakery / *be* a doctor / *be* a nurse

Let's Talk ❶

Work in pairs and talk about your work experience.

〈Example〉

> A : Where do you want to work in the work experience program?
>
> B : I want to work at a _____ .
>
> A : Why?
>
> B : I'm thinking of _____ .
>
>   *or*
>
> Because I _____ .

Toolbox A 〈workplace〉

レストラン	restaurant
ケーキ屋	cake shop
ペットショップ	pet shop
テレビ局	TV station
高齢者ホーム	home for the elderly

Toolbox B 〈reason〉 🔊

自分自身の＿＿店を開きたい	want to open my own _____ shop
高齢者を助けたい	want to help the elderly
動物が大好き	like animals very much
ジャーナリストに関心がある	*be* interested in being a journalist

📷 What do you see? Look at this photo and talk about it.

Let's Listen 2 🎧 🔊

Rikuya and Ayame are talking.

1. Check the correct boxes.

	Workplace			学んだこと		
Rikuya	① ☐	② ☐	③ ☐	④ ☐	⑤ ☐	⑥ ☐
Ayame	① ☐	② ☐	③ ☐	④ ☐	⑤ ☐	⑥ ☐

①

nursery school

②

restaurant

③

home for the elderly

④

Greetings are very important.

⑤

We should be kind to the elderly.

⑥
Teachers' work is very hard.

2. Work in pairs and check the answers.

(1) Where did [Rikuya / Ayame] go in the work experience program?

—— [He / She] went to _____.

(2) What has [Rikuya / Ayame] learned from [his / her] experience?

—— [He / She] has learned that _____.

Let's Read ❷ 🔊

Read Yumi's email to Eric and answer the questions.

> Hi Eric, how are you?
>
> Last month, the students in my class visited different workplaces to do some work there. My school has a work experience program. I helped in the pet shop near my house for two days. I cleaned the cages and water tanks there. The pets were very cute, and I've learned that we should be kind to animals.
>
> Your friend, Yumi

Words & Phrases 🔊

cages かご, おり   water tanks 水そう   I've = I have の短縮形   learned... …を学んだ

1. Where did Yumi work in the work experience program?

_____ .

2. What did she do there?

_____ .

3. What has she learned in the program?

_____ .

Let's Write ✏️

Where did you go in the work experience program? What have you learned?
 (Where do you want to go in the work experience program? Why?)

_____

_____

Let's Talk ❷

Work in pairs and ask your partner about the work experience.

Part 2 What do you want to be in the future?

Let's Listen ANSWER THE QUESTIONS 🔊

Yumi and Hayato are talking.

1. ☐ (a) A doctor

   ☐ (b) A nurse

   ☐ (c) A scientist

2. ☐ (a) Computers

   ☐ (b) Doctors

   ☐ (c) Science

3. ☐ (a) English

   ☐ (b) Math

   ☐ (c) Biology

Let's Read ❶ 📖 🔊

Hayato : What do you want to be in the future?

   Yumi : Well, I want to be a nurse.

Hayato : Why?

   Yumi : When I was a small child, I was in the hospital. At that time,

the nurses were very kind and helped me a lot.

Now, I want to help others as a nurse, too.

Hayato : That's great. I think you will be a good nurse.

   Yumi : Thank you. How about you, Hayato?

Hayato : I haven't decided yet, but I'm interested in science.

I want to study biology at university first.

   Yumi : I think you will be a great scientist.

Hayato : Thank you.

Words & Phrases 🔊

was in the hospital 入院していた　　　**as a nurse** 看護師として　　　**haven't decided yet** まだ決めていない

biology 生物　　　**scientist** 科学者

KEY PHRASES 🔊

What do you want to be in the future?

I want to be a nurse.

I haven't decided yet, but I'm interested in science.

Let's Practice

Work in pairs and practice the conversation between Hayato and Yumi.
Change roles.

Let's Talk ❶

Work in pairs and talk about a job that you are interested in.
Change roles.

〈 Example 〉

> A : What do you want to be in the future?
>
> B : I want to be _____ .
>
>   (I haven't decided yet, but I'm interested in _____ .)
>
> A : Why?
>
> B : Because _____ .

reporter

doctor

nurse

lawyer

teacher

computer
programmer

chef

(　　　)

Toolbox

病気の人を助ける	help sick people
困っている人を助ける	help people in need
新しいゲームを作る	make new games
お金をたくさんもうける	make a lot of money
自分のレストランを持つ	have my own restaurant
その仕事は社会で重要だ。	The job is important in society.
その仕事は人々を幸せにできる。	The job can make people happy.

Let's Read ❷ 📖 🔊

Read the passage with the graph and answer the questions.

Popular Jobs in Ms. Kimura's Class

Last week, Ms. Kimura talked with her students about jobs. The students are interested in different kinds of jobs. What is important when we are choosing a job? It is important to get information about jobs in many ways. For example, we can read books or ask someone about different jobs. Also, work experience is useful because we can learn many things about different workplaces. Ms. Kimura says that computer skills will be very important in many jobs.

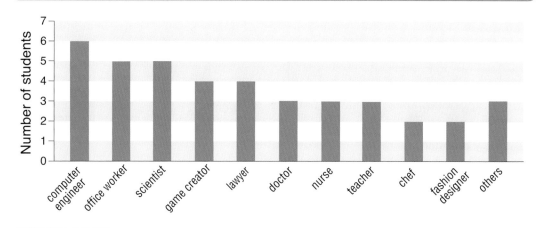

Words & Phrases 🔊

computer engineer コンピュータエンジニア   **game creator** ゲームクリエーター

in many ways 多くの方法で   **computer skills** コンピュータの技能

1. Which job is more popular in Ms. Kimura's class, "game creator" or "doctor"?

_____ .

2. What is important when we are choosing a job?

_____ .

3. Why is work experience useful?

_____ .

Let's Write ✏

What kind of job do you want to have in the future? Why?

_____

_____

_____

Let's Talk ❷

Work in groups of three or more. Talk about a job that [you want to have / you are interested in] and the reasons. Tell the class about your group's discussion.

〈Example〉

In our group, two students want to be game creators, one student wants to be a chef, and one student wants to be a teacher.

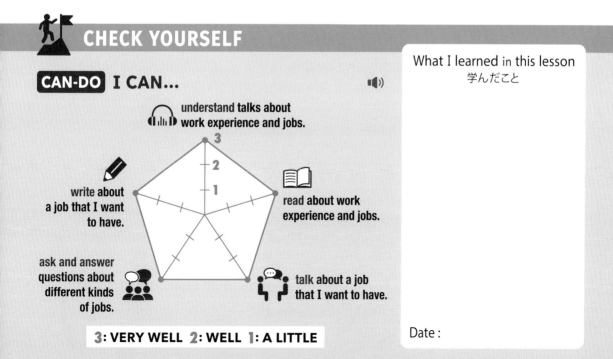

CHECK YOURSELF

CAN-DO I CAN... 🔊

understand **talks about** **work experience and jobs.**

3

2

1

write about a job that I want to have.

read **about work** **experience and jobs.**

ask and answer questions about different kinds of jobs.

talk about a job that I want to have.

3: VERY WELL 2: WELL 1: A LITTLE

What I learned in this lesson
学んだこと

Date :

Lesson 7

STAYING HEALTHY

CAN-DO In this lesson, you will...

 listen to talks about health problems and what to do with them.

 read about our body and health.

 talk about your health problems and what to do with them.

 ask and answer questions about ways to stay healthy.

 write about your health problems and what to do with them.

Part 1 I don't feel well this morning.

Let's Listen ❶ 🎧 ANSWER THE QUESTIONS 🔊

Hayato and the school nurse are talking.

1. He's ⬜︎ .

    ☐ (a) at home

    ☐ (b) in his classroom

    ☐ (c) in the school nurse's room

2. Because he doesn't feel ⬜︎

    ☐ (a) happy

    ☐ (b) hot

    ☐ (c) well

Let's Read ① 📖   🔊

Hayato : I don't feel well this morning. I'm sneezing and coughing,
and I can't breathe through my nose. My homeroom teacher
told me to come here.

Nurse : Did you take your temperature?

Hayato : No, I didn't. But I feel hot now. I have a sore throat, too.

Nurse : I think you have a slight cold.

Hayato : What shall I do?

Nurse : You should rest. Go home now. Don't stay up late.

Words & Phrases   🔊

sneeze くしゃみが出る   **cough** 咳が出る   **breathe** 呼吸する   **through** *one's* **nose** 鼻で

take *one's* **temperature** 体温を測る   **have a sore throat** のどが痛い

have a slight cold 軽い風邪をひいている   **rest** 休む

KEY PHRASES   🔊

You should rest.

Go home now.

Don't stay up late.

Let's Practice ① 👫

Practice the conversation between Hayato and the school nurse.
Change roles.

Let's Practice ❷

Practice the KEY PHRASES in pairs.
Change roles.

〈Example〉

A : I【   ①   】.

B : 【   ②   】

①	②
feel cold	You should rest.
have a fever	Go home now.
have a sore throat	Don't stay up late.
have a cough	Go to bed early.
have a runny nose	Take a nap.

Let's Talk ❶

Talk about a health problem and give advice.

〈 Example 〉

A : I have [a sore throat / a cough / a runny nose]. / I don't feel well.
/ I can't breathe through my nose well. / I feel [hot / cold].

B : Do you have a fever?

A : I don't know. _____ (*another problem with the body*),
too. What should I do?

B : I think you have a slight cold. (*advice*) (**Toolbox**)

Toolbox

今夜は早く寝なさい。	**Go to bed early tonight.**
体育の授業は出てはだめ。	**Don't attend the P.E. class.**
許可をもらって帰る方がいい。	**You should get permission to go home.**
今夜はお風呂に入るべきでない。	**You shouldn't take a bath tonight.**
様子を見よう。	**Let's see how it goes.**
しばらくここにいたら。	**Why don't you stay here for a while?**

📷 **What do you see?**　Look at this photo and talk about it.

Let's Listen ❷

Nanami and Ken are talking.

1. Check the correct phrase and fill in the blank.

(1) Why does Ken look tired?　　　　　　　〈look tired 疲れているように見える〉

—— It's because he was ⬚ last night.

☐ (a) doing homework

☐ (b) playing a game

☐ (c) preparing for an exam

☐ (d) sleeping at his desk

(2) What is Nanami's advice?

—— We become sick if we don't ＿＿＿＿＿＿＿＿＿＿ enough.

2. Work in pairs and check the answers.

(1) What did Ken have to do last night?

—— He had to ＿＿＿＿＿＿＿＿＿＿.

(2) What advice did Nanami give to Ken?

—— She said ＿＿＿＿＿＿＿＿＿＿.

Let's Read ❷ 📖

🔊

Read an article about our body and disease and answer the questions.

> Our body has a special ability. It can protect us against disease. So, if we lose this ability, we can become sick or tired easily. The cause of many illnesses is the damage to this ability or its loss. Doing exercise, getting enough sleep, eating healthy food, taking a bath, and laughing are examples of good ways to keep this ability and stay healthy.

Words & Phrases

🔊

ability 能力   **protect ~ against...** …から~を守る   **disease** 病気   **lose** 失う
cause 原因   **illness** 病気   **damage** 傷つけること, 損失   **loss** 失うこと, 喪失
stay healthy 健康でいる

1. How many examples of ways to stay healthy are given?

_____ .

2. Are you doing anything from these examples now?

_____ .

3. How do you say that special ability in Japanese?

_____ .

Let's Write ✏️

What do you usually do when you feel sick?

_____

_____

Let's Talk ❷

Work in pairs and discuss what you usually do when you feel sick.

Part 2 I'm afraid they may have the flu.

Let's Listen 🎧 ANSWER THE QUESTIONS 🔊

Hayato and Sayaka are talking.

1. They're talking about ☐☐☐ tomorrow.

   ☐ (a) the math test

   ☐ (b) the field trip

   ☐ (c) their club activities

2. They're going to ask their teachers to ☐☐☐.

   ☐ (a) cancel the club activities

   ☐ (b) plan a field trip

   ☐ (c) reschedule the math test

Let's Read ❶ 📖 ◀))

Hayato : I'm not ready for the math test tomorrow. I have had a headache since yesterday.

Sayaka : Nanami and some other students are absent today. I'm afraid they may have the flu. Maybe more students will be absent tomorrow.

Hayato : How about asking Ms. Mori and Mr. Ueno to reschedule the test?

Sayaka : Let's try it. Shall we go ask them right now? If they reschedule it, we need time to tell the other students about the change.

Hayato : That's right.... Ugh! I feel so sick.

Sayaka : Oh, no! You should skip your club activities today and go straight home. I'll go ask them.

Words & Phrases ◀))

have a headache 頭痛がする   **since yesterday** 昨日から   **flu** インフルエンザ

reschedule... …の計画を変える・延期する   **Let's try it.** やってみよう。   **go ask** 行って頼む, 頼みに行く

right now 今すぐに   **Ugh!** ごほん。   **feel so sick** とても気分が悪い   **skip** 休む

go straight home まっすぐに家に帰る

KEY PHRASES ◀))

How about asking Ms. Mori and Mr. Ueno to reschedule the test?

Shall we go ask them right now?

Let's Practice

Work in pairs and practice the conversation between Hayato and Sayaka.
Change roles.

Let's Talk ❶

Practice the conversation below with your classmates.
Change roles.

〈 Example 〉

> A : （ NAME ）, I have a headache. （ **Toolbox A , B** ）
>
> B : Are you OK? How about going to bed early? （ **Toolbox C** ）

Toolbox A	Toolbox B	Toolbox C
母 **Mom**	熱がある **have a fever**	保健室へ行く **going to the school nurse**
父 **Dad**	のどが痛い **have a sore throat**	温かい飲み物を飲む **having a hot drink**
保健室（養護教諭）の先生名 ［**School Nurse**］	咳がよく出る *be* **coughing a lot**	のどあめをなめる **taking a throat candy**
担任の先生名 ［**Your Homeroom Teacher**］	くしゃみがよく出る *be* **sneezing a lot**	体育の授業を休む **skipping your P.E. class**
友だちの名前 ［**Your Friend**］	気分が悪い *be* **feeling sick**	部活を休む **skipping your club activities**
	頭がふらつく *be* **feeling dizzy**	帰宅して休養する **going home and resting**
	具合がよくない *be* **not feeling well**	

Let's Read ❷ 📖 🔊

Read the passage with the graph and answer the questions.

Our Family Doctor

Dr. Sato is our family doctor. We consult her and ask for medical advice when someone in our family isn't feeling well. She knows us very well. She listens to us carefully and sometimes does some medical tests to find out the cause. However, she prescribes medicine or gives us injections only when it's necessary.

She says there is still no medicine to cure a common cold, but that our body has a natural ability to cure itself, even without medicine.

Also, before we leave her office, she always gives us some advice like, "When you get home, wash your hands and gargle well," or "Always eat well-balanced meals, and don't stay up late at night."

That way she helps us both feel and get better when we have health problems.

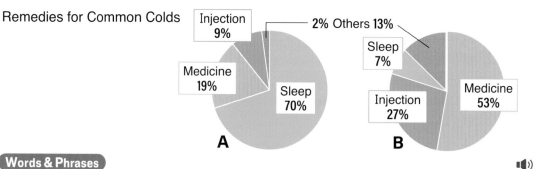

Remedies for Common Colds

A: Injection 9%, Medicine 19%, Sleep 70%, Others 2%
B: Sleep 7%, Others 13%, Injection 27%, Medicine 53%

Words & Phrases 🔊

remedy-remedies 対処法 　**consult...** …に診察してもらう 　**ask for...** …を求める

prescribe... …の処方箋を出す 　**injection** 注射 　**cure** *oneself* 自分で治す, 回復する 　**gargle** うがいをする

1. Why does Dr. Sato prescribe medicine or give injections only when necessary?

_____.

2. Which pie chart do you think shows Dr. Sato's remedies, A or B?

_____.

3. Do you have a family doctor? Are your doctor's remedies closer to A or B?

_____.

Let's Write

Write about what you are doing to stay healthy or build up your strength, or what you do when you don't feel well.

_____

_____

_____

Let's Talk ❷

Work in groups of three or more and talk about what you wrote above. Tell the class about your group's discussion.

⟨Example⟩

_____ usually _____ when [he / she] _____.

(*Feel free to add other interesting information:* _____.)

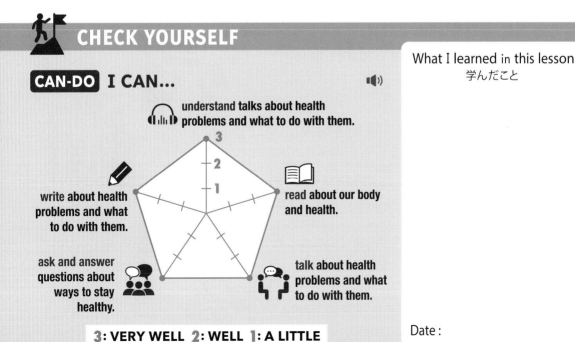

CHECK YOURSELF

CAN-DO I CAN...

understand **talks about health problems and what to do with them.**

read about our body and health.

write **about health problems and what to do with them.**

ask and answer **questions about ways to stay healthy.**

talk **about health problems and what to do with them.**

3: VERY WELL 2: WELL 1: A LITTLE

What I learned in this lesson
学んだこと

Date :

Lesson 8

MUSIC AND YOUR FREE TIME

CAN-DO In this lesson, you will...

 listen to talks about music and free time.

 read about music and free time.

 talk about music and free time.

 ask and answer questions about music and free time.

 write about music and free time.

Part 1 — What do you usually do in your free time?

Let's Listen ① ANSWER THE QUESTIONS

Meg and Rikuya are talking.

1. Meg [　　　].

   ☐ (a) is interested in what Rikuya does in his free time

   ☐ (b) doesn't use her smartphone to listen to music

   ☐ (c) usually listens to music on the internet radio

2. Rikuya likes to [　　　].

   ☐ (a) watch a lot of videos in his room

   ☐ (b) read books and magazines at home

   ☐ (c) listen to music on his smartphone

Let's Read ❶ 📖 🔊

Meg : What do you usually do in your free time?

Rikuya : I love listening to music on my smartphone.

Meg : Me, too. We can enjoy any kind of music anywhere with it. What else do you do?

Rikuya : When I don't feel like doing anything, I just listen to music on the internet radio. How about you, Meg?

Meg : At home, I watch a lot of television, and I read a lot of comic books.

Rikuya : I have some comic books I don't read anymore. Would you like them?

Meg : Sure!

Words & Phrases 🔊

in *one's* **free time** 自由な時間のあるときに   **anywhere** どこにいても   **Would you like...?** …は要りますか。

KEY PHRASES 🔊

What do you usually do in your free time?

I always listen to music on my smartphone.

Let's Practice ❶ 👥

Work in pairs and practice the conversation between Meg and Rikuya.
Change roles.

Let's Practice 2

Work in pairs and ask your partner about free time.
Change roles.

〈Example〉

A : What do you do in your free time?

B : I【 ① 】【 ② 】【 ③ 】.

①	②	③
always	listen to music	at home
almost always	play computer games	in the library
usually	go (out) for a walk	in the park
often	read books or magazines	on my smartphone
sometimes	watch TV or videos	with my friends
	Your ideas:	Your ideas:

Let's Talk ❶

Work in pairs and talk about music.
Change roles.

〈 Example 〉

> A： What kind of music do you listen to in your free time?
>
> B： I usually listen to ＿＿＿＿＿＿. （**Toolbox A**）
>
> A： Do you use an audio player or your smartphone for that?
>
> B： I [always / usually / sometimes] ＿＿＿＿＿＿. （**Toolbox B**）

Toolbox A

日本のポップス	J-pop（Japanese popular music）	フォーク	folk music
韓国のポップス	K-pop（Korean popular music）	クラシック	classical music
ボーカロイド	vocaloid music	ゴスペル	gospel music
ダンスミュージック	dance music	ジャズ	jazz
イージーリスニング	easy listening music	ロック	rock

Toolbox B

スマホを使う	use my smartphone
インターネットを使う	use the internet
ラジオで音楽番組を聞く	listen to music programs on the radio
テレビで音楽番組を見る	watch music programs on TV
インターネットで音楽ビデオを見る	watch music videos on the internet

📷 **What do you see?** Look at this photo and talk about it.

Let's Listen ❷ ■))

Ayame and Jon are talking.

1. Choose the correct sentences about Jon and Ayame.

   ☐ (a) Jon is good at singing.

   ☐ (b) Jon is very worried about the music festival.

   ☐ (c) Ayame doesn't know anything about mixed chorus.

   ☐ (d) Ayame wants Jon to join her group.

2. Work in pairs and check the answers.

   (1) What is Jon going to do at their music festival?

   —— He hasn't decided yet. He likes _____, but he can't _____.

   (2) What is "mixed chorus"?

   —— _____ and _____ sing together in a mixed chorus.

   (3) Is Jon interested in joining Ayame's group?

   —— _____.

Let's Read ❷ 📖 🔊

Read a story about music in Greentown and answer the questions.

> People in Greentown are all music-lovers. Some people like lively music, while others prefer quiet music. They listen to music when they're happy, sad, or tired. They enjoy listening to all kinds of music in their free time, from classical to anime songs. Some people listen to music while studying or working, too.
>
> However, they not only listen to music but also love to play music and sing. There are many opportunities to learn, practice, and perform music. Everyone enjoys music in Greentown.

Words & Phrases 🔊

music-lovers 音楽好き **lively music** 軽快な音楽 **prefer...** …の方が好きだ **worried** 不安で

anime songs アニメの歌 **opportunity - opportunities** 機会

1. What kind of music do the people in Greentown like?

_____.

2. Which do they prefer, listening to music or playing music?

_____.

3. Imagine you are living in Greentown now. What would you do in your free time?

_____.

Let's Write ✏️

Write about what music you want to listen to in your free time.

_____

_____

Let's Talk ❷

Work in pairs and discuss what you usually do when you have some free time on weekends.

Part 2 — What will take the place of radios or TVs in the future?

Let's Listen ANSWER THE QUESTIONS

Nanami and her grandfather Akio are talking in a car.

1. Nanami ⬚ .

☐ (a) has never seen cassette tapes before

☐ (b) doesn't know anything about music on the internet

☐ (c) wants to buy a new tape recorder for her father

2. Akio ⬚ .

☐ (a) enjoyed music on his computer when he was young

☐ (b) doesn't have any cassettes or tape recorders now

☐ (c) was happy to hear his favorite song on the radio

Let's Read ❶ 📖 🔊

Akio : Nanami, who's singing this song on the radio now?

Nanami : Sugiyama Miku. Don't you know her? She's one of the most popular singers now.

Akio : Is she? You know, this is a song I liked very much when I was your age.

Nanami : Is that right? How did you know that song? You didn't have any internet then, did you?

Akio : Of course not. A radio and a cassette tape recorder were the only devices we had at that time.

Nanami : Cassettes? I've heard of them but never seen or listened to one before. Do you still use them?

Akio : No, but I kept one player and a lot of my favorite cassette tapes. They're in a box in my room. I haven't listened to them in years, but they're my treasure.

Nanami : Let's listen to them sometime. I guess people of all ages enjoy listening to music, even though the machines change over the years.

Akio : I wonder what will take the place of radios in the future.

Words & Phrases 🔊

when I was your age あなたと同じ年齢のとき   **cassette tape recorder** カセットテープレコーダー
devices 機器   **sometime** いつかそのうち   **take the place of...** …の代わりとなる

KEY PHRASES 🔊

Who's singing this song on the radio now?
I've heard of them but I've never seen or listened to one before.

Let's Practice

Work in pairs and practice the conversation between Akio and Nanami.
Change roles.

Let's Talk ❶

Work in pairs. Talk about what you do in your free time.
Change roles.

〈 Example 〉

> A : What do you usually do after school?
>
> B : I (always / usually / sometimes) _____ . (**Toolbox A**)
>
> How about you?
>
> A : Me? I'm busy after school. I _____ . (**Toolbox A**)
>
> B : Then how about in your free time?
>
> A : I _____ . (**Toolbox B**)
>
> B : I see.

Toolbox A

クラブ活動がある	have club activities（activity-activities）
ダンスを習う	have dance［class/practice］
バレエを習う	have ballet［class/practice］
塾に通う	go to cram school
ピアノの練習をする	practice the piano
友だちと遊ぶ	hang out with my friends
家の手伝いをする	help at home

Toolbox B

本やマンガ, 雑誌を読む	read books, manga, or magazines
インターネットを使う	use the internet
コンピュータゲームをする	play computer games
音楽を聞く	listen to music
買い物に行く	go shopping
テレビを見る	watch TV
映画を見る	go see a movie

Let's Read ❷ 📖   🔊

Read the passage with the graph and answer the questions.

An Internet Survey: Students' Use of Time After School

Students around the country spend a lot of time on their smartphones and computers these days.

Here is a summary of the results from a recent internet survey of 1,000 junior and senior high school students about their use of time after school.

They spend about 1 hour and 30 minutes using different kinds of media every day, but they average less than 20 minutes playing with their friends.

You will be surprised to see the average number of hours 3rd year junior high school students spend on studying. It is 3 hours and 20 minutes, the highest in the chart. Even the 3rd year students at senior high school only study for 2 hours and 30 minutes.

How long do you study every day? What do you do in your free time?

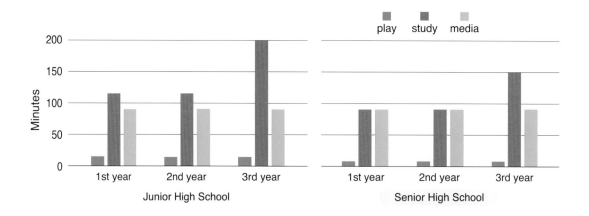

1. How long do the 2nd year students at junior high schools spend using media?

_____ .

2. Which group of students study the longest?

_____ .

3. How much time do you want to spend on music every day? Why?

_____ .

Let's Write

Choose either A or B, and write about it.

A. What kind of music do you want to listen to when you're free? Why?

B. What kind of musical instrument do you want to learn to play? Why?

Let's Talk ❷

Work in groups of three or more and talk about A and/or B above. Tell the class about your group's discussion.

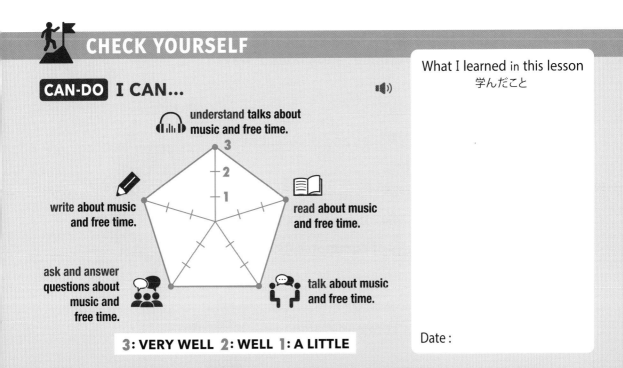

CHECK YOURSELF

CAN-DO **I CAN...**

understand **talks** about music and free time.

read **about** music and free time.

talk about music and free time.

ask and answer questions about music and free time.

write **about** music and free time.

3: VERY WELL 2: WELL 1: A LITTLE

What I learned in this lesson
学んだこと

Date :

Lesson 9

SMARTPHONES AS PART OF LIFE

CAN-DO In this lesson, you will...

 listen to talks about smartphones and different ways of communication.

 read about smartphones and different ways of communication.

 talk about smartphones and different ways of communication.

 ask and answer questions about smartphones and different ways of communication.

 write about smartphones and different ways of communication.

Part 1 We can do many things with smartphones.

Let's Listen ❶ ANSWER THE QUESTIONS ◀))

Yumi and Jon are talking.

1. ☐ (a) 30 minutes

   ☐ (b) 1 hour

   ☐ (c) 2 hours

2. He ☐☐☐ his friends in Canada.

   ☐ (a) sends messages to

   ☐ (b) talks with

   ☐ (c) plays online games with

Let's Read ❶ 📖 🔊

Yumi : Wow, you finally got a smartphone!

Jon : Yes, my parents bought it for me. But I can only use it for two hours a day. Also, I can't play online games.

Yumi : That's too bad. What do you do with your smartphone then?

Jon : I often send messages to my friends in Canada. I want to talk to them, but it's difficult because of the time difference between Japan and Canada. I listen to music and watch videos of my favorite musicians, too. You can do many things. You can even study English!

Yumi : Really? How?

Jon : There are many apps for learning English words.

Yumi : That's great. I hope my parents will buy one for me soon!

Words & Phrases 🔊

two hours a day 1日に2時間　　online games オンラインゲーム

time difference between Japan and Canada 日本とカナダの時差　　even... …でさえ　　apps アプリ

KEY PHRASES 🔊

What do you do with your smartphone?

I often send messages to my friends in Canada.

Let's Practice ❶ 👫

Work in pairs and practice the conversation between Yumi and Jon.
Change roles.

Let's Practice ❷ 👥

Work in pairs and talk about computers, cellphones, or smartphones.
Change roles.

〈Example〉

> A : What do you do with your _____?
>
> B : I（often）_____.

listen to music / watch videos / read the news / search for information /
send messages / take pictures / play games

Let's Talk ❶

Work in pairs and talk about your use of smartphones.

〈 Example 〉

A : Do you have a smartphone?

B : Yes, I do.

A : How long do you usually use it in a day?

B : I use it for ＿＿＿＿＿ a day.

A : What do you do with your smartphone?

B : I（ often ）＿＿＿＿＿＿＿.

（**Toolbox A**）

A : Do you have a smartphone?

B : No, I don't.

A : Do you want a smartphone?

B : ＿＿＿＿＿＿＿＿＿.

A : Why?

B : Because ＿＿＿＿＿＿＿.

（**Toolbox B**）

Toolbox A

天気を調べる	check the weather
電車の時刻表を調べる	check the train schedule
自分の写真をとる	take selfies
たくさんアプリを使う	use many apps
友だちにメールを送る	text my friends

Toolbox B

今は必要ない。	I don't need it now.
みんなが持っている	everyone has one
高い	it's expensive
使うのが難しい	it's difficult to use

📷 **What do you see?** Look at this photo and talk about it.

Let's Listen ❷ 🎧   🔊

Yumi and Mr. King are talking.

1. What does Mr. King do with his smartphone? Choose three things.

☐ listen to music

☐ read newspapers

☐ study Japanese

☐ talk with family and friends

☐ take pictures

☐ play games

2. Work in pairs and check the answers.

（1）What does Mr. King do with his smartphone?

⎯ He _____.

（2）What does Mr. King have for pets?

⎯ He has _____ for pets.

（3）What does Mr. King do every morning?

⎯ He _____ every morning.

Let's Read ❷ 📖 🔊

Read the school news article and answer the questions.

Tips for Smart Use of Your Smartphone

Smartphones are popular because they are very useful, but using them for a long time is bad for your health. For example, you can hurt your eyes and your neck muscles. Follow these smartphone rules for a healthier life.

1. Don't use your smartphone while eating.

2. Don't use your smartphone for more than three hours a day.

3. Don't use your smartphone just before you go to bed.

Words & Phrases 🔊

tips ヒント　　hurt... …を痛める　　neck muscles 首の筋肉　　follow 従う

healthier より健康な（healthy の比較級）　　while eating 食事中

1. Why are smartphones popular?

_____ .

2. What are health problems caused by smartphones?

_____ .

3. If you use your smartphone just before you go to bed, what might happen?

_____ .

Let's Write ✏️

Do you have a smartphone?　　☐　Yes. → What do you do with it?

　　　　　　　　　　　　　　☐　No. → Do you want one? Why or why not?

Let's Talk ❷ 💬

Work in pairs and talk about your use of smartphones.

Part 2   Do you send New Year's cards?

Let's Listen ANSWER THE QUESTIONS 🔊

Jon and Ayame are talking.

1. She ⬚ them.

   ☐ (a) calls

   ☐ (b) sends letters to

   ☐ (c) sends text messages to

2. He wants to send ⬚ to his friends and relatives.

   ☐ (a) cards

   ☐ (b) presents

   ☐ (c) both cards and presents

Let's Read ❶ 📖 🔊

Jon :　Now we can use computers, cellphones, or smartphones to communicate. Thanks to the development of technology, we can communicate with people all over the world easily. But in the past, people sent postcards or letters.

Ayame :　Yeah, my grandmother still keeps old love letters from my grandfather.

Jon :　That's really nice. How about you? Do you write letters or send postcards sometimes?

Ayame :　No, I don't. I'm not good at writing letters. Also, it takes a long time for letters to arrive.

Jon :　How do you communicate with your friends? Do you often call them?

Ayame :　No, I always send text messages with my smartphone. It's easy and quick.　How about you, Jon?

Jon :　Now that I have my new smartphone, I'll probably send a lot of text messages. But I still want to send Christmas cards to my friends and relatives. And I think I want to keep calling them on their birthday, too.

Ayame :　My grandmother still sends midsummer and New Year's cards to all our relatives and many of her friends.

Words & Phrases 🔊

thanks to... …のおかげで　　**development of technology** テクノロジーの発展　　**in the past** 過去に
now that... 今や…だから　　**relatives** 親戚

KEY PHRASES 🔊

Now we can use computers, cellphones, or smartphones to communicate.
It takes a long time for letters to arrive.

Let's Practice

Work in pairs and practice the conversation between Jon and Ayame.
Change roles.

Let's Talk ❶ 💬

Work in pairs and talk about how to communicate with your family and friends. Change roles.

〈 Example 〉

> A： How do you communicate with your family and friends?
>
> B： I _____ . (**Toolbox A**)
>
> A： Do you send birthday cards, Christmas cards, or New Year's cards?
>
> B： _____ .
>
> A： ［ Why? / Why not? ］
>
> B： Because _____ . (**Toolbox B**)

Toolbox A 🔊

メールを送る	send text messages
電話で話す	talk on the phone
ビデオ電話をする	have video calls with them
会って話す	meet and talk with them

Toolbox B

友だちと連絡を取るのに良い方法だ。	It is a good way to keep in touch with friends.
カードを作るのはおもしろい。	It is fun to make cards.
独創的なことをするのを楽しむ。	I enjoy doing something creative.
友だちはカードを見るのが好き。	My friends like looking at the cards.
面倒くさい。	It's too much bother.
買って送るのは高くつく。	It's expensive to buy and send.

Let's Read ❷ 📖 🔊

Read the report with the graph and answer the questions.

New Year's Cards

Every year in January since 1990, a Japanese information company has been making a survey about New Year's cards.

According to the summary of the survey, sending New Year's cards has become less popular. However, some people still send New Year's cards because it is a traditional Japanese custom. It is also a good way to greet friends and acquaintances.

Even so, other people don't send New Year's cards because it is troublesome or expensive. They often send emails or short messages for their New Year's greetings.

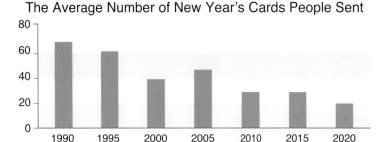

The Average Number of New Year's Cards People Sent

Words & Phrases 🔊

custom 習慣　　**greet** あいさつをする　　**acquaintance** 知人　　**even so** そうは言っても
troublesome 面倒な　　**New Year's greetings** 新年のあいさつ

1. What is the average number of New Year's cards people sent in 2000?

   _____.

2. Why do some people send New Year's cards?

   _____.

3. What are other ways to make New Year's greetings?

   _____.

Let's Write ✏

Do you send New Year's cards every year? If you do, do you make them yourself or buy them? If you don't, why not? Write the reason(s).

_____

_____

_____

Let's Talk ❷ 🗪

Work in groups of three or more and talk about New Year's cards. Tell the class about your group's discussion.

⟨Example⟩

In our group, _____ send New Year's cards.

And _____ of them make their own cards.

_____ don't send New Year's cards because _____ .

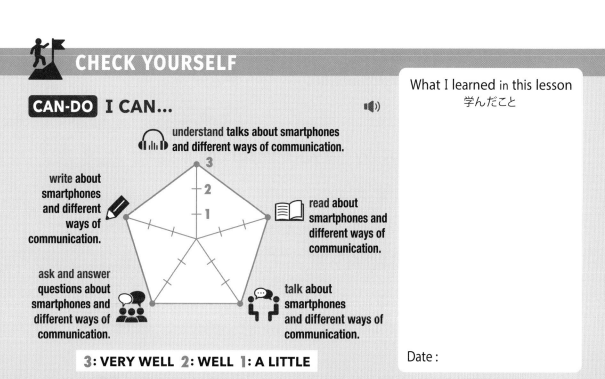

🏃 CHECK YOURSELF

CAN-DO **I CAN...** 🔊

understand **talks about smartphones and different ways of communication.**

write **about smartphones and different ways of communication.**

read **about smartphones and different ways of communication.**

ask and answer **questions about smartphones and different ways of communication.**

talk **about smartphones and different ways of communication.**

3: VERY WELL 2: WELL 1: A LITTLE

What I learned in this lesson
学んだこと

Date :

Lesson 10

EXPERIENCES IN A FOREIGN COUNTRY

CAN-DO In this lesson, you will...

 listen to talks about foreign countries.

 read about foreign countries.

 talk about the country that you want to study in.

 ask and answer questions about the country that you want to study in.

 write about the country that you want to study in.

Part 1 I want to try Japanese tea ceremony.

Let's Listen ❶   ANSWER THE QUESTIONS ◀))

Eric and Nanami are talking.

1. They went to ⬚ .

   ☐ (a) Australia

   ☐ (b) a festival

   ☐ (c) a tea ceremony

2. He will ⬚ .

   ☐ (a) go swimming

   ☐ (b) drink tea at a festival

   ☐ (c) visit the tea ceremony club

Let's Read ❶ 📖 🔊

Nanami : That's a beautiful picture, Eric.

Eric : Yes, it's a picture of the Great Barrier Reef in Australia.
I went there with my family last year. I love swimming.

Nanami : Me, too. I went to Izu last summer. The ocean was clear and
cool. So, is there anything you want to do in Japan?

Eric : Yes. I want to try Japanese tea ceremony. I drank some
green tea at a festival before, and it was delicious. It was
held in a traditional Japanese tearoom.

Nanami : Sure. We can visit the tea ceremony club after school.

Eric : Sounds great. I'll be looking forward to it.

Words & Phrases 🔊

ocean 海　　**tea ceremony** 茶道　　*be* **held in...** …で開催される

KEY PHRASES 🔊

Is there anything you want to...?

Yes. I want to...

Let's Practice ❶ 👥

Work in pairs and practice the conversation between Nanami and Eric.
Change roles.

Let's Practice ❷ 👫

Work in pairs and talk about Japanese experiences.
Change roles.

〈Example〉

> A : Is there anything you want to do in Japan?
>
> B : Yes. I want to <u>eat sushi at a fish market</u>.

---

climb Mt. Fuji	eat delicious food(s) in Osaka
go shopping in Shopping Street	wear *yukata* at a festival
travel around by train	Your ideas :

Let's Talk ❶

Work in pairs and talk about what you want to do.

〈Example〉

A : Is there anything you want to ＿＿＿＿＿＿ ? （Toolbox A）

B : Yes. I want to ＿＿＿＿＿＿＿＿＿＿ . （Toolbox B）

A : Why?

B : Because ＿＿＿＿＿＿＿＿＿＿ . （Toolbox C）

Toolbox A

see in Tokyo / do in Harajuku / eat in Osaka / do in Hokkaido / try in Okinawa
Your ideas :

Toolbox B

watch *rakugo* at a theater
go shopping in Harajuku
eat *takoyaki* in Osaka
see beautiful nature in Hokkaido
try diving in Okinawa
Your ideas :

Toolbox C

It looks interesting.
I want to buy cool clothes.
It's a popular food.
I'm interested in wild animals.
I like swimming in the ocean.
Your ideas :

📷 **What do you see?** Look at this photo and talk about it.

Let's Listen ❷ 🎧 ◀))

Nanami and Eric are talking.

1. Choose the answers.

   (1) What club did Eric visit?

 ☐  ☐  ☐  ☐

   (2) Why does Eric want to try Kendo?

   Because [ ]

   ☐ (a) he likes fencing

   ☐ (b) it teaches politeness and respect

   ☐ (c) he wants to try a Japanese sport

2. Work in pairs and check the answers.

   (1) What did Eric think about his club experience?

   —— He thought it _____.

   (2) What club does he want to experience next?

   —— He wants to try _____.

Let's Read ❷ 🔊

Read Eric's email to his parents in Singapore and answer the questions.

> Hi Mom and Dad,
>
> How's everything back home? It's been three months since I arrived here in Japan. I'm having a great time with my host family and school. I spend a lot of time studying Japanese at home and at school.
>
> Last weekend I went to a Japanese festival. There, I ate octopus for the first time. It was called *takoyaki*. It's a small golf-ball-shaped food made of flour, eggs, and cabbage. There are small pieces of octopus in the middle. You eat it with a brown sauce and mayonnaise. It was very different, but it was delicious.
>
> There are so many things I want to tell you. I'll write to you about my school next time.
>
> Eric

Words & Phrases 🔊

... -shaped …の形をした   *be* **made of...** …でできている

1. How long has Eric been in Japan?

_____ .

2. What did Eric do at the Japanese festival?

_____ .

3. Did Eric like *takoyaki*?

_____ .

Let's Write ✏️

Write an email to a student abroad. Introduce one traditional Japanese thing.

_____

_____

Let's Talk ❷

Work in pairs and read your email to your partner.

Part 2 Are you interested in studying abroad?

Let's Listen ANSWER THE QUESTIONS

Jon and Nanami are talking.

1. Because she ☐

   ☐ (a) wants to eat cakes and scones

   ☐ (b) is interested in studying in the U.K.

   ☐ (c) likes to look at pictures of flowers

2. He ☐ .

   ☐ (a) thinks that they are beautiful

   ☐ (b) likes food more than gardens

   ☐ (c) wants to have a garden, too

Let's Read ❶ 📖   🔊

Jon : Hi Nanami. What are you reading?

Nanami : Hello Jon. Oh, this is a guidebook to the U.K. I borrowed it from the school library. It has a lot of information about the history and culture of the country. The pictures are really nice, too.

Jon : Really? Can I see them?

Nanami : Sure. Look, this page is about afternoon tea in London.

Jon : Wow! The cakes and sandwiches on these plates look really delicious. Are you interested in studying there?

Nanami : Yes. I'm interested in the food and gardens. Look at this page about English gardens. These flowers are so beautiful, aren't they?

Jon : Umm. Yes, I guess so. But sorry, I'm not into flowers that much. I would rather have cakes and scones with English tea.

Nanami : Ha, ha. That's what I thought.

Words & Phrases   🔊

be into... …が大好きで   **I would rather...** 私はむしろ…   **scone-scones** スコーン

KEY PHRASES   🔊

Are you interested in...?

Yes. I'm interested in the food and gardens.

Let's Practice

Work in pairs and practice the conversation between Jon and Nanami.
Change roles.

Let's Talk ❶

Work in pairs and talk about a country you are interested in studying in.
Change roles.

〈 Example 〉

> A : Are you interested in studying in _____ ?
>
> B : [Yes / No].
>
> A : Why?
>
> B : Because _____ .

Singapore

see the Merlion

Egypt

visit the pyramids

Canada

go to Niagara Falls

Australia

learn about wild
animals

France

go up the Eiffel
Tower

U.S.A.

explore the Grand
Canyon

China

walk on the Great
Wall

Italy

make delicious
pizza

Let's Read ❷ 📖 🔊

Read the passage with the graph and answer the questions.

Studying Abroad

Are you interested in studying abroad? Here are the results of my class survey: "What country do you want to study in?"

The most popular choice was Canada. It's a multicultural country with people from many different backgrounds. Many students want to experience living with a Canadian host family. You can also learn French as a second language at school.

The second most popular country was France. Three out of seven want to become pastry chefs. The other students are interested in fashion.

The U.K. and the U.S.A. were the third most popular destinations for students interested in studying music and drama. They want to be able to sing and perform in musicals in English.

The same number of students chose the Philippines and Singapore because they are close to Japan. Finally, two students wanted to study about environmental issues in Australia, especially how to save endangered animals.

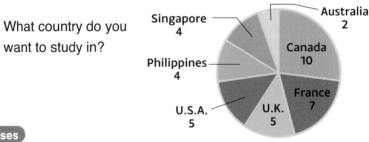

What country do you want to study in?

Singapore 4 · Australia 2 · Canada 10 · Philippines 4 · France 7 · U.S.A. 5 · U.K. 5

🔊

Words & Phrases

multicultural 多文化の　　**... out of ~** ~のうち…　　**pastry chef** パティシエ　　**pastry-pastries** 焼き菓子

destinations 目的地　　**environmental issues** 環境問題　　**endangered** 絶滅の危機にさらされた

1. What did the students want to experience in Canada?

_____ .

2. How many students want to study music and drama?

_____ .

3. Where did the two students want to study about environmental issues?

_____ .

Let's Write

Imagine you're going to study abroad next year. Write about your plan at your new school in that country.

_____

_____

_____

_____

Let's Talk ❷

Work in groups of three or more and talk about your plan above. Tell the class about your group's discussion.

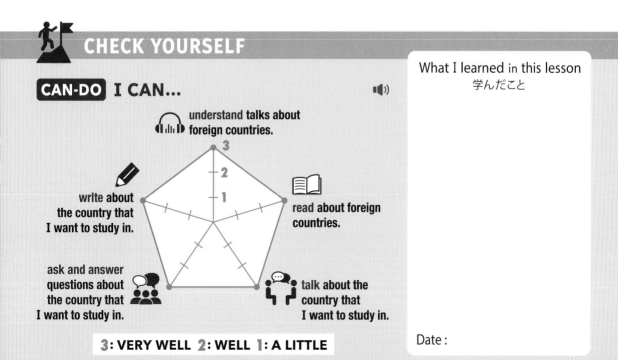

【著者】
　高田三夫
　石川和弘
　柳瀬和明
　柳田恵美子
　萱忠義
　齋藤雪絵
　Colette Morin

【編集・執筆協力】
　佐伯林規江

【表紙デザイン・イラスト】
　デザインスタジオ・maru　丸田薫

【本文デザイン】
　京都文英堂　株式会社　反保文江

【ウェブディレクター】
　株式会社　office masui　益井貴生

【音声編集】
　シンプティースタジオ　粕谷和弘

写真提供
　アドビ　株式会社
　株式会社　アマナイメージズ

Open Seas for Global Friendships II

2023 年 10 月 1 日　　第 1 刷発行

監修者　上智大学名誉教授　吉田　研作
　　　　上智大学教授　　　藤田　保

発行所　京都文英堂株式会社
　　　　〒601-8372　京都市南区吉祥院嶋高町12番地
　　　　（代表）075-661-9960

販　売　株式会社　文英堂

印刷所　株式会社　天理時報社

What do you see?

A PET AS A FAMILY MEMBER ①

FOOD PREFERENCES ②

③ MEANS OF TRANSPORTATION

④ TOO HOT

⑤ ONLINE MEDIA

⑥ WORK EXPERIENCE AND JOBS